The Boar's Head Theatre

The Boar's Head Theatre

An Inn-yard Theatre of the Elizabethan Age

by
the late C. J. Sisson, *Charles Jasper 1885 - 1966.*
formerly Professor of English, University of London

edited by Stanley Wells
Shakespeare Institute, University of Birmingham

Routledge & Kegan Paul

London and Boston

First published 1972
by Routledge & Kegan Paul Ltd
Broadway House, 68–74 Carter Lane,
London EC4V 5EL and
9 Park Street,
Boston, Mass. 02108, U.S.A.
Printed in Great Britain by
Alden & Mowbray Ltd
at the Alden Press, Oxford

ISBN 0 7100 7252 X

for

Vera Sisson

and

Rosemary Anne Sisson

Contents

Figures

Editor's Introduction

C. J. Sisson, Lord Northcliffe Professor of English Language and Literature in the University of London from 1928 to 1951, editor of Shakespeare, and author of several books and many articles on Elizabethan life and literature, was an indefatigable searcher of archives. He worked especially in the Public Record Office, where he discovered many lawsuits involving writers, actors, and other figures interesting in relation to theatrical and literary history. Among his discoveries were papers concerned with the Boar's Head Inn, and with its use as a theatre. He published a short account of this in *Life and Letters Today*[1] called 'Mr and Mrs Browne of the Boar's Head'. This was intended for the general reader. Partly for this reason, and partly, no doubt, because he intended to produce later a fuller, scholarly account, he cited no references.

Not long afterwards came the Second World War, during which Professor Sisson's library and notes were destroyed. This, along with work on his complete edition of Shakespeare, which appeared in 1954, delayed him in the difficult task of resuming work on the Boar's Head. Also in 1954 he published an article[2] in which he touched on the topic, identifying some of his references. Leslie Hotson briefly discussed inn-yard theatres, including the Boar's Head, in *Shakespeare's Wooden O*, 1959, and Sisson discusses Hotson's work in Appendix A.

In his retirement, Sisson wrote up his discoveries in substantially the form in which they appear here. The lucidity of his account disguises the difficulty of his task. The documents from which he

[1] Vol. 15, no. 6, winter 1936, pp. 99–107.
[2] 'The Red Bull Company and the Importunate Widow', *Shakespeare Survey 7*, 1954, pp. 57–68.

worked do not present the facts in anything approaching chrono-logical order, and the work of organising them was a considerable challenge to a man in failing health, even one as experienced in reading records as Sisson. When he died, in 1966, few people knew that he had completed a book on the subject.

My association with Professor Sisson dates back to a day in 1947 when, as a schoolboy, I travelled from Yorkshire to London as an applicant for a place in the English Department of University College, and was interviewed by him in his room in Foster Court. During my years as an undergraduate I attended his lectures on Shakespeare, and also his classes in palaeography, in which he was assisted by his ever-loyal colleague, Miss Winifred Husbands, his assistant editor on the *Modern Language Review*. I attended the dinner given for him on his retirement in 1951, when I too left University College. Sisson, still full of energy, joined the Shakespeare Institute in Stratford-upon-Avon as Senior Fellow.

Our paths converged again when, in 1958, I joined the Institute as a graduate student. Here, naturally, my contact with him was closer than when I was an undergraduate. I remember him at the weekly seminars, presided over by Allardyce Nicoll, and attended also by another authority on the Elizabethan theatre, I. A. Shapiro. They were a varied trio: Nicoll elegant, unfailingly courteous, attentive to the opinions even of the least experienced student, steering the discussions with his infallible tact, relieving the occasional difficult situation with a dry Scottish wit; Shapiro, strong in argument, im-placable in his logic, scrupulous in his regard for evidence; and Sisson, the oldest of the three, but also the most mischievous, ripe in sagacity, genial in his capacity for irreverence, his generosity of response, his obvious warmth of heart. A twinkle lurked always behind his gold-rimmed glasses, which he used like an actor, peering over them to make a point or to launch a quip. No one who knew him will forget how he would roll his own cigarettes, nasty little objects that he rarely succeeded in smoking without needing to relight them several times.

In his seventy-fourth year he retired again, and it was understood that now he would be able to complete his work on the Boar's Head. I was, I suppose, the only one of his students to be present at both his retirement parties. The one in Stratford was held at his charming house in Tyler Street, and Mrs Inga-Stina Ewbank, who at that time was a Fellow of the Institute, cooked a boar's head to mark the occasion. He went to live in Sussex, then in London. He maintained connections with the Institute, coming to Stratford occasionally to lecture or for the International Shakespeare Conference. The last time I saw him, I asked about his work on the Boar's Head, but he was despondent about it, feeling that it would never be completed.

Not long after his death, in 1966, his widow did me the honour of asking me to look through his papers to see if he had left anything that should be published. It was pleasant to find that his lengthy retirement had given him the opportunity to write up and to publish most of the interesting material that he had discovered in the public records. And I was surprised and delighted to learn that a complete typescript existed of a book on the Boar's Head. This had been entrusted to the care of another scholar, but pressure of work prevented him from doing anything about it, and some years later Mrs Sisson asked me if I would prepare it for publication. I was pleased to undertake the task, though bad luck still attended the book since illness prevented me from completing it as quickly as I should have liked.

Though the typescript was complete, there were some puzzles of the kind that would probably have been resolved by the author as the book went through the printing process. Editorial work was obviously required. Furthermore, two scholars had published material that touches on the content of this book, Professor Glynne Wickham writing on inn-yard theatres in general, and Professor Herbert Berry on the Boar's Head in particular. It seems desirable to offer some account of their work.

In Volume One (1959) of his *Early English Stages: 1300 to 1600*, Professor Wickham warns us of the danger of drawing analogies between the appearance of inn-yards and public theatres (pp. 5–6). In his second volume, he expresses scepticism about the evidence on which those who have considered inn-yards as a probable source of influence on public theatres have seen 'fit to set performances at inns so firmly in the yard', and suggests that when theatrical performances were given at inns they are much more likely to have been in halls or galleries rather than in the yards. It is clear that Professor Wickham did not know Sisson's 1936 article, and that he would have written differently if the present book had been available to him.

Professor Berry, of the University of Saskatchewan, has published a substantial article called 'The Playhouse in the Boar's Head Inn, Whitechapel'.[1] He intends to publish other articles on different aspects of the same topic, and perhaps to gather his findings into a book. Professor Berry has not seen the typescript of this book, though of course he knows Sisson's earlier article on the same topic, and also had available to him the references to some of the material given in Sisson's article in *Shakespeare Survey 7*. Sisson's book is larger in scope than the work so far published by Professor Berry. Sisson sets the new information about the Boar's Head in a wider social and theatrical context, and offers more subsidiary material. So far as the Boar's Head itself is concerned, Professor Berry shows knowledge of one or two relevant cases that were not known to Sisson, but the bulk of their information derives from the same central documents. There are some interesting discrepancies between their findings, resulting largely from the complexity of the material and the fact that it is in some respects open to variety of interpretation.

Their conclusions about the location and structure of the inn are very similar. Professor Sisson made many rough sketches of the layout of the Boar's Head. Clearly, and understandably, he experienced problems in precisely interpreting the evidence. Some of his sketches include a stage, and it is clear that, as the verbal evidence demands, he envisaged the stage against the west wall. The two plans reproduced on pages xv, xvi are based on those made by Professor Sisson, and the evidence presented in his book. Berry's plan of the rooms on the ground floor differs from Sisson's mainly in assuming

[1] In David Galloway, ed., *The Elizabethan Theatre: Papers given at the International Conference on Elizabethan Theatre held at the University of Waterloo, Ontario, in July, 1968*, 1969, pp. 45–73.

that the hall to the west of the entrance led straight into a parlour and kitchen, all on the south side of the rectangle occupied by the buildings. Sisson places the parlour and kitchen in the west wing. Sisson seems to consider that a garden and backyard lay beyond the great barn which closed the north end of the building; Berry places a small yard at the north end of the west wing itself. Both Sisson and Berry (like Hotson) place the stage along the west wall. Sisson's text is not explicit on this point, but his draft sketches show it there. Berry (p. 49) thinks that the stage was not already in the yard when Woodlif took over, but Sisson, giving rather more evidence (pp. 4, 8, 36), suggests the likelihood that stage and tiring house already existed in 1594. The two scholars express opposed views about the existence of an upper acting area, Sisson believing that one was available when required (p. xix), Berry that it was not (p. 55). The evidence seems inconclusive.

A matter in which Berry appears to correct Sisson relates to the companies using the inn as a theatre. Berry (pp. 67, 68 n.) thinks that there were two companies, Derby's and Worcester's, whereas Sisson takes it that these are a joint company. Sisson provides a convincing explanation (p. 67 n.) of an apparent discrepancy in statements by Langley and Samwell (see Berry, p. 59).

As will be apparent, Herbert Berry's carefully considered and scholarly article is indispensable to the study of this topic. The differences of opinion between Sisson and him may in some cases reflect unresolvable ambiguities in the evidence. If so, the publication of Sisson's views will usefully draw attention to areas in which certainty is still not attainable. It is possible, too, that Professor Berry will be in a position to adduce additional evidence in support of his own interpretations.

In preparing Sisson's typescript for the press, I have checked the quotations from printed sources, and supplied a few additional references. I have not attempted to follow fully Sisson's footsteps in his researches. In no case have I modified his treatment of the evidence. I have checked quotations from the more important legal documents, of which Sisson's photostats are on deposit in the Palaeography

Room of the Goldsmiths' Library, University of London. Sisson fills in the picture with details derived from many subsidiary sources; I have not thought it necessary to verify these. The only warning that needs to be given is that Sisson sometimes omitted stereotyped legal formulae, such as 'the said deponent', from his quotations. I have modernised the spelling and punctuation of all the quotations, and expanded contractions, though I have left proper names in the forms preferred by Sisson (e.g. 'Samwell', which Hotson modernises to 'Samuel', and 'Poley', which Berry gives as 'Pooley'). The plans have been prepared under my supervision, and I am responsible for the index. I am grateful for assistance with the proofs from Mr R. L. Smallwood.

As I worked I have, of course, been wary of doing anything of which the author would have disapproved. Probably I have not succeeded, but I feel at least that I have acted as he would have wished in my choice of dedicatees.

S.W.

Figure I Ground Floor

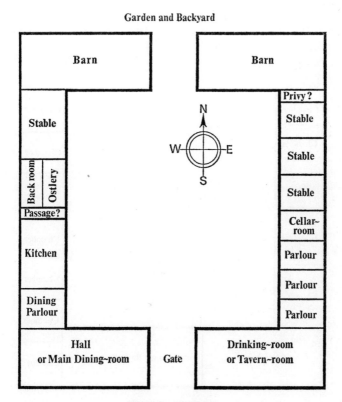

Garden and Backyard

Whitechapel Street

Figure II Upper Storey

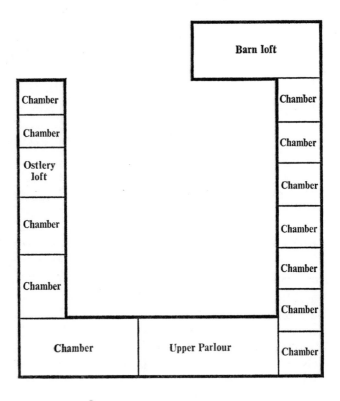

Introduction

The Boar's Head Theatre is briefly reported by Sir Edmund Chambers, in his monumental *The Elizabethan Stage*,[1] as a 'short-lived house of which practically nothing is known' (II, 366). In fact, its history spans a period of over fifty years, from 1557 to 1608 at least, and with further knowledge it emerges as an important and exceptionally interesting theatre.

Moreover, despite Chambers's denial (II, 444), it was beyond all question an inn-yard theatre. The trend of recent thought has been increasingly opposed to the theory that inn-yards provided the structural origins of Elizabethan public play-houses, favouring rather the design of bear-baiting or bull-baiting arenas, or of stage-patterns derived from the use of halls at Court or University, or from the pageant-houses of medieval miracle-plays, and even from analogies with Spanish usages. The Boar's Head now presents the picture of a permanent stage-structure erected within the area of an inn-yard, with tiring rooms and stands for the accommodation of spectators—and this at the peak period of Shakespeare's activity in the Elizabethan stage and drama. There is little doubt that the Red Bull Theatre was similarly an inn converted to theatrical purposes. The commonly assumed concept of removable trestle-stages as the sole structural provision of inn-yard theatres must be abandoned, and with it the notion of the galleries or balconies of inn-chambers as the spectators' only alternative to standing in the yard. The concept is indeed discredited by more careful consideration of what we have long known

[1] E. K. Chambers, *The Elizabethan Stage*, four vols., 1923.

(from a document of 1567) about the Red Lion Theatre, which, like the Boar's Head, was a Whitechapel inn-theatre, close to the City.

This information strongly suggests, in fact, a continuous link between inn-yard theatres and other public theatres. An unbroken history leads from the Boar's Head in 1557 and the Red Lion ten years later to the Theatre of 1576, a proposed new George Inn Theatre in 1580, now first recorded, and so through the Swan and the later Boar's Head on to the Globe, the Fortune, and the Red Bull. The first pioneer of the Elizabethan theatre, John Brayne, was financier of the Red Lion in 1567 and, with James Burbage, of the Theatre in 1576. He was almost certainly associated with Burbage and Leicester's Men in the Red Lion venture. After the Theatre, he moved towards a further inn-yard theatre project in Whitechapel, the George Inn. The Theatre itself, transferred from Shoreditch to Bankside, gave birth to the Globe under the direction of Burbage, Brayne's close associate and brother-in-law, and in due course Burbage's Globe served in part as model for Edward Alleyn's Fortune Theatre. Alleyn had begun his 'prentice career as actor with Robert Browne, leader of Worcester's Men, in 1583 and a veteran of the days of inn-yard theatres, who designed and financed the elaborate development of the Boar's Head Inn as a permanent theatre. Later on, Francis Langley, builder of the Swan Theatre on Bankside, added this inn-yard theatre to his investments in the stage, as we now learn. It is impossible to maintain that the designers of the Theatre, the Globe, or the Fortune, were indifferent to the traditions and structures of the inn-yard theatre.

The long-established classical concept of the main structures of the Elizabethan public stage has come under heavy fire, and doubt has been cast upon the very existence of the supposed inner stage and upper stage. The tiring rooms have even been relegated in one account to the cellar under the stage, to serve the concept of an 'arena stage'.[1] Discussion of the inner stage or 'study' has been lamentably bemused by the delusion that action set there must be confined within its area and is incapable of extending from this focus to the main stage which thereupon partakes of its location. The

---

[1] Leslie Hotson, *Shakespeare's Wooden O*, 1959, Chapter 4.

well-known sketch-drawing of the Swan stage, which shows no central opening in the stage-wall, has led to the concept of tented structures to serve the purpose of 'study'-scenes. Some kind of upper stage is obviously indicated in stage-directions and in the vocabulary of the stage, and it must have been located in the gallery over the stage, a structure which cannot be denied and is vouched for at the Boar's Head. Recent enquiries have reasonably questioned the exclusive appropriation of a certain part of this gallery for this purpose. Less reasonably, it has been held to be entirely appropriated to superior seating accommodation for spectators, with other provisions proposed for action 'above', again in the interests of the 'arena' stage. There is no doubt that there was a conflict between the convenience of its use as part of the stage and its value to the sharers as a kind of dress-circle for spectators. It has been observed that action 'above' is required much less frequently than we may have imagined, indeed only in about one half of the plays available for study. The inference would seem plain: that part of this gallery would be reserved when required by the action of the play to be performed; otherwise all of it would be available for spectators.

In view of these questions, and of many others raised in the great volume of recent scholarly discussions of the stage, the discovery of any further contemporary descriptions of an Elizabethan theatre is of exceptional interest, and an account of the structure of the Boar's Head Theatre contributes much material for their reconsideration. We learn also a good deal about the managerial arrangements of a theatre erected in an inn-yard setting, and about its finance, not least about the burden of a great variety of claims upon its resources, including heavy impositions by outside interests. The financial importance of the gallery above the stage is manifest at the Boar's Head, as is also the necessity of tiring houses and of an inner stage which can open and close.

New information leads also to revision of the biographical history of two notable figures, John Brayne, the true 'first builder of playhouses' (a phrase applied to James Burbage by his son Cuthbert), and Robert Browne, builder of the Boar's Head, leader of Worcester's Men in 1583, travelling actor in Germany, and a stalwart of the

Elizabethan theatre-world, of whom hitherto only the most confused and fragmentary accounts have been given. Among the financiers of the theatre, new figures emerge—those of Richard Samwell and Oliver Woodlif—and Francis Langley's investments in the theatre increase in importance.

Apart from all these matters of interest in theatrical history, we have what is perhaps the most complete and detailed written record of the nature and the precise layout of the accommodation provided by a large London inn in 1594. Sketch plans of the inn may for the first time claim the authenticity of a basis in contemporary documentary evidence.

The story of the Boar's Head Theatre is enlivened by its emergence from an intimate picture of Whitechapel dwellers, and by conflicts between rival landlords which led to riotous proceedings in the theatre itself in the midst of a performance. The consequent insecurity for a famous company of actors who occupied Browne's theatre was the probable cause of their breach of an agreement with him to confine their activities to his theatre and of their departure to Henslowe's Rose Theatre. The whole story makes it entirely comprehensible why Robert Browne, 'Browne of the Boar's Head', as Mrs Joan Alleyn wrote to her husband in 1603, 'died very poor'.

Finally, we are compelled to reconsider the significance of the famous City inns, for so long the centres of the professional stage and drama in London. The evidence points to the conclusion that permanent stages and stands for spectators were erected in their yards, as at the Boar's Head, and that in this true sense those inns were converted to theatres, and served as London headquarters for companies of actors, until in 1596 the City authorities closed those that fell under their jurisdiction.[1]

[1] See Chambers, *The Elizabethan Stage*, II, pp. 359–60.

Chapter I

The Inn-yard Theatre

The four fundamental requirements for the actors' profession are a stage, a tiring room, accommodation for spectators, and control of their access to the performance. It might be well to approach the question of the significance of inn-yards in the history and structure of the Elizabethan public theatre in the light of these simple considerations, which were foremost in the minds of the first builders of theatres.

The professional theatre developed its importance in English life during the reign of Queen Elizabeth I, at her Court, and in the City of London and its suburbs. The Theatre, founded in 1576, was the first building designed solely for the purposes of a theatrical company. But it seems clear that a group of large City inns were already in use as theatres, possibly (as Chambers hints)[1] by established companies of actors, and with permanent facilities for acting in their yards. Early records of two Whitechapel inns, the Boar's Head in 1557, and the Red Lion in 1567, certify the use of suburban houses also as theatres. The innkeeper and the actor alike, after all, were in the business of entertainment, and each served the other's purposes and brought him custom. Good cheer and the drama were old friends in London, from the days early in the sixteenth century when the feasts of the great City Companies were followed by a play to complete the day's amusement.[2] We can hardly be content with accounts of the

---

[1] Chambers, *The Elizabethan Stage*, II, pp. 356–7, supported by Flecknoe's account in 1664, cited by Chambers.
[2] See for example the unpublished records of the Drapers' Company, *passim*.

great companies of actors which record only performances at Court and in the provinces, and offer no suggestions as to James Burbage's London headquarters, as leader of Leicester's Men, before the building of the Theatre. His patent of 1574 specifically licensed him to play 'within our City of London',[1] a phrase which plainly suggests an inn-yard theatre as his headquarters, and as the setting for professional acting to which he was accustomed.

The first and third of the actors' requirements, the stage and room for spectators, could well be provided for by structures in an inn-yard to supplement the mere use of the yard as standing-room, resembling the balconies or galleries on the first floor leading to the inn-chambers. There is evidence of such provision at the Red Lion in Whitechapel as early as in 1567. Tiring rooms, the second essential of a public theatre satisfactory to a company of actors which had passed beyond the outlook of a parcel of mountebanks, are not specifically mentioned in any inn-yard theatre until we come to consider the Boar's Head Theatre, where they were an integral part of the structure. As for the fourth essential, the necessary control of the entrance of spectators upon payment at the door, the Elizabethan inn-yard provided an admirable pattern for the design of a theatre to meet this requirement.

The means to these ends were readily provided by the layout of a yard designed to meet the needs of travellers and carriers. An enclosed rectangular space of considerable area, surrounded by buildings, had an entrance gate for horses and for wagons which unloaded in the yard. The wagons, unwieldy without bogey-wheels, were unable to turn in a limited space or in a full yard, and made their way out at the far gate of the yard opposite the entrance. Horses were put up in stables which formed part of the surrounding buildings, with access from the yard. Closure of both entrance and exit gates assured the safety of horses and wagons with their loads in the enclosed yard. When the inn was converted to theatrical uses, the exit gate was closed, and the entrance gate controlled. With a permanent stage and scaffolds, the yard and its exit would be obstructed by these erections, a complete impediment to the traffic of carriers and their wagons. The closure of the exit gate assured control by 'gatherers' at the entrance

[1] Chambers, op. cit., II, p. 87.

gate, as the principal means of public access to the yard, and this power to close the entrance is specifically provided for at the Boar's Head during the hours of performances.

The obvious place for tiring rooms was behind the stage, with means of access by openings upon the stage, one possibly high and wide enough to serve the purpose of inner stage or 'study' scenes. With galleries for spectators erected over the stage, the privileged tiring-house door into the theatre, for which there is ample evidence, would be shared by the actors and by spectators prepared to pay higher prices for superior accommodation and for a privileged entry. The Swan drawing, which shows the *mimorum aedes* behind the stage-wall, clearly supports this location of the tiring rooms deduced from the practical consideration of convenience in an inn-yard theatre, as it also shows beyond reasonable doubt a gallery over the stage occupied by spectators.

It follows that an inn with permanent structures and used regularly for theatrical purposes could no longer cater for the heavy traffic of a carriers' inn, though it could perhaps manage horse traffic with riders and loads, and could continue to provide food and drink, and possibly even lodging and ostler-service for its customers. It is evident, therefore, that further information upon the history of London inns in their relation to such traffic might well throw light upon the history of the stage in London. It is not without significance, for example, that the heavy traffic in East Anglian cloth was directed by Elizabethan regulations away from inn-yards to the city depot in Blackwall for inspection and disposal, a beginning of the system of great central markets in London.[1] The Whitechapel inns consequently came to have no need to house the wagons coming by the eastern approaches from Essex and Suffolk with their loads of cloth. But the adequate entertainment of clothiers, their wagoners and horsemen, continued to be an increasing concern of innkeepers. The partial closure of the yard permitted the development of theatrical entertainments in close association with the inns, with facilities that could satisfy the rising standards and increasing elaboration of the play as a form of art.

It is now evident that a new conception of the inn-yard theatre

[1] See the evidence of Francis Langley: Star Chamber 5, A8/4, 1599.

emerges into view, and that it is at variance with the accepted account in stage-history of the inn-yard as a port of call for companies of actors in the provinces or for more frequent use in certain inns in the City of London, under conditions of improvisation proper to an establishment engaged mainly in the normal traffic of an inn. The improvised inn-yard performances of plays may well belong not to the history of the London stage from the reign of Elizabeth onwards, but rather to an earlier and more elementary form of dramatic entertainment. Little is known about such performances. Travelling companies in the provinces are recorded as performing mainly in guild-halls or in great houses, though there is evidence that they also used inns for this purpose.[1] As for the London inns, it may be that when they emerge into stage-history they had in some measure provided their yards with permanent structures. The Boar's Head of 1557, in the last year of Mary's reign, may have resembled the Red Lion, also in Whitechapel, with similar structures. Certainly it had such structures before 1594, as appears from the new material concerning what might be called the Second Boar's Head. If the evidence reflects in some measure upon the history of the inn-yard theatre, its significance is perhaps even greater in relation to the history and structure of the public theatre.

We may reasonably single out John Brayne as the first recorded pioneer in the history of the stage to see the possibilities of the development and the elaboration of the inn-yard theatre, which may have usurped upon the inn-yards of London inns known for dramatic activities to a degree far beyond present conceptions of their functions. It is easy to underestimate the extent of the structures erected by him in the Red Lion inn-yard in Whitechapel in 1567, as recorded in the well-known entry in the Court-Book of the Carpenters' Company.[2] At first sight Brayne's controversy with the carpenter William Sylvester suggests a modest transaction, involving a sum of only £8. 10s. But the question at issue is the improvements required to work already done, to satisfy the demands of those concerned with

---

[1] As with Worcester's Men at Norwich under Robert Browne, including Alleyn, in June 1583: Chambers, op. cit., II, pp. 222–3.
[2] Quoted in Chambers, op. cit., II, pp. 379–80.

4

staging plays in the yard; probably, in fact, the demands of James Burbage and Leicester's Men, the most prominent company of the day. It is plain that the whole transaction was of considerable scope, and that the sum of £8. 10s. was only the amount of an outstanding and final instalment of payment by Brayne to Sylvester. Sylvester had set up 'scaffolds', as the record reports, and it is reasonable to interpret the word 'scaffolds' in the plural as including both a stage and structures for spectators in the yard, the word bearing both these meanings in common use. There is every reason for holding that Brayne's Red Lion Theatre provided in the inn-yard some structures of a permanent nature. The stage provisions which the carpenter had improved upon Brayne's orders were inaugurated by the performance of the play of *Sampson*, when Brayne and the actors were satisfied by the amended structures. He then paid the balance of his debt to Sylvester, returned his bonds, closed his books, and his theatre came to life.

When we consider not only these facts but also Brayne's later history, this seems a far more probable interpretation of the record than the suggestion that we are concerned here only with the provision at a total cost of £8. 10s. of an elaborate scenic structure as a setting for the feats of strength that form part of the story of Samson, valid only for that one production. The history of the Boar's Head at a later date relates a similar dissatisfaction with its original stage-structures, with provision for extending them at a further cost. It is credible that in both cases there was a need to satisfy the company of actors whom it was desired to attach to the theatre, Leicester's Men at the Red Lion and Worcester's at the Boar's Head.

Brayne's transactions with the Red Lion Inn in 1567 assume vastly greater significance in the light of his association as partner with James Burbage in the foundation and building of the Theatre in Shoreditch in 1576, only nine years after his erection of a theatre with 'scaffolds' in a Whitechapel inn. We know that Burbage had married Brayne's sister Ellen, and that their elder son, Cuthbert, was born in 1566–7, in the year of Brayne's development of the Red Lion. We know too that James was the leader of Leicester's Men in 1572 and 1574, and probably in 1567, when he was thirty-six years of age. It is reasonably certain that he and his company used Brayne's Red Lion as their London theatre, and that its foundation arose out of consultation between Brayne and Burbage.[1] Their partnership moved on from the Red Lion in Whitechapel to the next parish, adjoining St Mary's Whitechapel in the north, St Leonard's Shoreditch, where they built their new theatre. We cannot doubt that in the design of the new theatre both partners came to their task mindful of their experience in this earlier venture.

Four years later, it now appears,[2] Brayne embarked upon a third venture as a builder of theatres, with his acquisition of the George Inn in Whitechapel in 1580, an investment of which the purpose has not emerged in previous accounts of the transaction. It is significant that Brayne, despite his experience with Burbage and the Theatre in Shoreditch, now returned to Whitechapel and to the conversion of an inn into a theatre, as with the Red Lion in 1567. The design of a theatre built upon open ground solely for histrionic purposes, it seems, was not incompatible with that of a further conversion of an inn-yard for similar purposes.

The history of the Red Bull Theatre in Clerkenwell some twenty years later points in the same direction. The examination of extant documents bearing upon the Red Bull leaves little question that here again we have an inn converted into a theatre, as indeed its name suggests. The evidence of further documents, for example the depositions in Chancery in 1623[3], bears out the conclusion supported by the description of the property in Thomas Woodford's Bill:

> one messuage or tenement with the appurtenances commonly called and known by the name of the Red Bull situate in the parish of St James Clerkenwell ... [in which Aaron Holland] did afterwards erect, build, and set up in and upon some part of the same messuage or tenement divers and sundry buildings and galleries [which he afterwards] leased for a playhouse [for acting]

---

[1] Fleay's suggestion, reported by Chambers, op. cit., II, p. 380, that Leicester's Men used the Bull Inn from 1560 to 1576, rests upon untenable identifications of plays and is unacceptable.

[2] See Chapter II below, and Appendix B.

[3] See C. J. Sisson, 'The Red Bull Company and the Importunate Widow', *Shakespeare Survey 7*, 1954, pp. 57–68.

and [setting] forth of plays, comedies, and tragedies, or to do
other exercises at and in the same.[1]

If this 'messuage' was not an inn, we are left with the impossibility of
any alternative suggestion. Holland's buildings were erected within
the premises already in existence. The 'open part' of the 'messuage'
certainly suggests the yard or 'court' of an inn, in which Holland set
up 'buildings and galleries'. Holland's 'buildings', as distinct from
his 'galleries', suggest equally plainly stage and tiring rooms as
distinct from stands for spectators. The terms of his description of the
property, with its 'court' and 'cellars', offer a close parallel to those
used in reference to the Boar's Head.

We have been too ready to accept the assumption that the history
of the Red Bull as a theatre begins about 1605 with Holland's development of the site. We have on record the statement in 1623 of the actor
John King, a member of Worcester's–Queen Anne's Men, that he
has been in constant employment with the company for over thirty
years:

> for the space of these 30 years past and upwards he hath been a
> hired servant unto the company of sharers of the players of the
> Red Bull, and saith that when this deponent came first to be
> entertained in the said house [and company] the then sharers did
> agree with him this deponent to give him wages certain by the
> week.[2]

King thus takes us back to a date before 1593 for his beginning at the
'house' of the Red Bull. We cannot ignore the specific statement,
especially when the 'company' is apparently an afterthought in his
evidence. He was forty-eight years of age in 1623, and presumably
began his career with the company before he was eighteen years of
age.[3] His acquaintance with Susan Baskerville began at the same time,
as he tells us. She was then Susan Browne, second wife of Robert

---

[1] Modernised from 'Three London Theatres of Shakespeare's Time', by
C. W. Wallace, in *Nebraska University Studies*, IX, 1909, p. 303.
[2] C24/500/103; deposition of John King, of the parish of St Sepulchre, London,
gentleman, aged forty-eight. The words 'and company' are an interlined addition.
[3] Alleyn began with Worcester's Men before he was seventeen.

Browne, leader of Worcester's Men. There is thus reason for the belief that there was an inn-yard theatre at the Red Bull from at least 1593, and that Worcester's Men used it before they moved to the new Boar's Head in Whitechapel. It is perhaps significant that they moved back, as the Queen's Men, from the Rose to Holland's new Red Bull when it was completed.

It is also significant that Aaron Holland, builder of this theatre, was an innkeeper,[1] and yet another link in the continuous connection of the building of theatres with the usages and structures of inns. It is well to recall further that Edward Alleyn was the son of an innkeeper in St Botolph's and nephew to the elder Edward's successor in his inn.[2] Alleyn began his career as an actor with Robert Browne's company, Worcester's Men, the company which is most closely connected with the Boar's Head Theatre, and which acted in inns at Norwich in 1583.

It is clear that the Boar's Head Inn-Theatre already had permanent structures like those of the Red Lion before 1594 when it again emerges in documentary records. There are references in the accounts of its rebuilding to the resiting of its former stage, and to an 'old long gallery' which was pulled down when galleries were erected on a larger scale. The inn-yard theatres of London were plainly not satisfied with temporary, improvised, removable accommodation for stage-plays. Some of the most notable figures in the history of the Elizabethan stage were closely associated with London inns and with their use for theatrical purposes, which surely presented a shadow-pattern for the designing of new theatres in London.

The actors and their financiers, after all, were engaged in extending the business of the inns and their keepers: the business of entertaining the public. Certainly there was co-operation between the two wings of this industry, not least in the provision of facilities for the exercise

---

[1] Sessions Rolls, Guildhall 355/38, June 1598: 'innholder in the Savoy'. In 1589 and 1592 he is recorded as living in Gray's Inn Lane (C24/228/47; E 179/269/41). He gives his age as sixty-seven on 3 February 1623, then living in St James Clerkenwell (C24/497/Bingham *v* Bonham). He signs, with difficulty, the initials 'A.H.'.

[2] On 23 January 1578, John Allen, orphan of Edward Alleyn, innholder, was 'boarded' by the City with William Rawson, innholder (City of London, *Repertories* 19, f. 280 v.).

of the actor's art. It is entirely explicable that two innkeepers, Richard Samwell of the Boar's Head and Aaron Holland of the Red Bull, should be associated with the financing of improved theatres in their inns. Companies of actors had difficulty sometimes in finding a suitable theatre for the practice of their profession. But the landlords of theatres were also dependent upon the companies for the provision of entertainment in their theatres and for the resultant share in takings which gave them a return upon their investments. The purchase of a lease of the property and the erection of structures for theatrical purposes involved them in a capital outlay of considerable magnitude, sometimes exceeding their expectations and their means, as possibly with Brayne at the Red Lion and certainly at the later Boar's Head. It might be expected that there would be co-operation between financier and actor, as there was between Brayne and Burbage at the Theatre. The relations between Holland and Thomas Swinnerton at the Red Bull arouse curiosity. On what consideration did Holland give Swinnerton a one-seventh part in the house, which Swinnerton was able to sell for £50? Swinnerton was not the leader of Queen Anne's Men, nor was he their manager. As compared with John Duke and Christopher Beeston he was a relatively unimportant member of the company. We can hardly believe that the company, seeking a suitable theatre, invested in Holland's venture through Swinnerton. But we may well believe that Swinnerton himself took a speculative part in financing the Red Bull, fortified by knowledge that his company would occupy the theatre upon its completion, and that he took his profit at once from the sale of his share, a share in the house as distinct from a share in the company, to Philip Stone, who sold it to Thomas Woodford in 1612–13.[1]

We have well-known records of the leaders of companies of actors entering into bonds to landlords, with a penalty for deserting their theatres. The history of the later Boar's Head adds another instance, with consequent legal proceedings. It is evident that the

---

[1] Stone was a London haberdasher, son of William Stone, a wealthy haberdasher whose second wife was Alice, the widow of John Day the printer, and who died in 1594–5 (C24/181/Day *v* Day; C24/244/72, C24/246/74, both Stone *v* Stone). William had an extensive estate at Segenhoe, Bedfordshire, as well as his London house and business.

landlord of an inn with permanent structures would be in a better position to bargain with a company of actors than one who could merely offer the hospitality of his yard for occasional performances on an improvised and removable trestle-stage. For the latter, the normal business of an inn would continue to be his principal concern and his chief source of income, and for this his yard must continue to be available, with only the added attraction of occasional plays. But with the impediment of stage-structures in permanent occupation of the yard, the landlord would obviously depend for his livelihood to a greater degree upon the use of his inn for theatrical purposes as a constant activity. It was only upon this condition that the inn-yard theatre could satisfy the actors' main requirements for the developing professional stage. The conclusion is irresistible, and all we know about the London inn-yard theatres bears it out: that this condition was fulfilled in a number of London and suburban inns before the foundation of the Theatre in 1576 by Burbage and Brayne.

We thus see the stage in such inns in transition from a means of entertainment ancillary to an older trade, as it was ancillary in early Tudor days to the feasts of the Lord Mayor or of the great City Companies and on its way towards an independent status in its own right and in its own buildings, as in the Theatre. As the Elizabethan drama grew from childhood to manhood in the inn-yard theatres of London, so surely the Elizabethan theatre emerged in its structures from the examples set and experienced in the exploitation of the great inn-yards of London as the paramount influence in the minds of the theatre-builders and of the companies of actors for whose use they were built. Information is now available on the actual structures erected within the yard of the Boar's Head for occupation by an important company of actors during the great age of the Elizabethan theatre and drama, and it is conclusive, showing the existence of the complete facilities of stage, tiring house, galleries for spectators, and full control of access, all the requisites of the mature theatre and drama.

There are indications, as might be expected, that the development of permanent structures in inns for theatrical purposes tended to affect inns which were no longer sufficiently prosperous in their traditional function, by loss of custom or through structural decay in old buildings requiring too great expenditure to justify repair or rebuilding. When the necessary capital could be found, there might be more promise of profit in providing for the growing trade of the stage, which moreover, if exercised in the inn, would increase custom on the tavern side of its activities and its dining-parlours. It may well be that the Red Lion and the Red Bull were falling out of prosperity. It seems clear that the Boar's Head was in this condition. And there is no doubt whatever that this is the picture that emerges from the story of a third Whitechapel inn, the George, which was also John Brayne's third venture into the theatre-world in the thirteen years from 1567 to 1580.

It would seem in fact that with the Red Lion, the George, and the Boar's Head, we are in presence of a theatre-district of limited area within the parish of Whitechapel, east of Aldgate bars and west of St Mary's Parish Church. Red Lion Street, on the south of Whitechapel Street, lay opposite to Boar's Head Yard to the north. Some three hundred yards to the east, also on the north of Whitechapel Street, lay George Yard, some two hundred yards west of the church.[1] The attraction of the area was plainly its proximity to the City, with facility of access for citizens and comparative freedom from control, as well as the crowded and increasing populousness of Whitechapel itself and the traffic of the main highway from London to the east. The district had the advantage over the group of inn-theatres in Bishopsgate and Gracechurch Street that it was not subject to the control of the City authorities. A brief account of Brayne's proposed George Inn Theatre may serve as a prologue to the full story of the Boar's Head.

[1] As shown in the map of the parish of Whitechapel in Stow's *Survey of London*, ed. John Strype, 1720, II, p. 44.

Chapter II

The George Inn in Whitechapel

The George Inn in Whitechapel has an importance in theatrical history beyond anything that may appear in the account given by C. W. Wallace in 1913 of John Brayne's acquisition of this property, which offers no explanation of Brayne's interest in it.[1] Wallace makes the daunting claim to have 'reached all documents of first importance in the public archives . . . for the Tudor–Stuart period of stage-history' (p. 34). He was not, however, aware that the George Inn had any relation to stage-history, and the Boar's Head also escaped his researches. The significance of Brayne's investment in the George Inn lies firstly in a project for a third inn-yard theatre to be set up in Whitechapel. Secondly, Wallace's account of the relations between Brayne, Burbage, and Miles, which has dictated the views set forth by Chambers and his successors upon transactions concerning the theatre as between Brayne and Burbage, rests upon the acceptance of highly prejudiced *ex parte* statements of Miles in his legal crusade against Burbage. With fuller information from further documents, the story throws a different light upon the activities of these two founders of the Elizabethan theatre. The view here taken is supported by a detailed examination of the complex series of transactions and consequent litigation (discussed in Appendix B) in which Miles involved Brayne and Mrs Brayne, and from which he emerges as a disreputable intriguer of exceptional dishonesty. The story inciden-

---

[1] C. W. Wallace, 'The First London Theatre', in *Nebraska University Studies*, XII, 1913, p. 106. The spellings of Brayne and Miles are established in use. In State Papers Domestic Elizabeth I, CXLVI, 31, Brayne signs 'By me John Brayne', but Miles 'By me Robart Milles'. His son George, however, signs 'George Miles' in C24/314/86, and his son Ralph 'per me Raphe Miles'.

tally furnishes an unexpected footnote to discussion of the date of Shakespeare's *Romeo and Juliet*.

The site of the George Inn is indicated by early maps which show George Yard entering Whitechapel Street on the north side, some three hundred yards east of Boar's Head Yard. Like the Boar's Head, it lay within the Manor of Stepney. Its first discoverable owner was John Field, who in the first year of Elizabeth held it in customary fee from the Manor. Its first recorded landlord was John Biggs, to whom in 1559 Field leased the inn, with ground adjoining and with the Mill House, for twenty-one years at an annual rental of £7. Biggs died before the expiry of his lease, leaving it to his wife, who married Reinold Rogers. The inn by now was in need of extensive repairs, and Rogers refused to seek the renewal of his lease before its expiry in 1580. Field thereupon granted a new lease of the inn for twenty-five years at a rental of £30 to John Brayne on 12 January 1580.[1]

We may well be puzzled by such an investment, in which the financial risks are evident enough, with a heavy rental charge and little apparent return to justify Brayne in venturing where Rogers had retreated in dismay. Rogers and his wife had full knowledge of the property and its possibilities as an inn from their own experience as lessees. But nothing was further from Brayne's mind than investment in an inn as a going concern in its normal functions.

The project upon which Brayne embarked was in fact to convert the George Inn into a new theatre. Four years before, Brayne had engaged with Burbage in the foundation of the Theatre in Shoreditch. The new project, encouraged by the prosperity of its predecessor, was a sequel to this venture. It was, indeed, Brayne's third incursion into the same field of investment, his first so far as we know being the financing of the Red Lion, also in Whitechapel. It is perhaps significant that this third venture, like his first, was the conversion of a large inn into a theatre. Despite his experience of a theatre built and designed from the ground in Shoreditch, Brayne evidently still conceived of an inn and its yard as furnishing a suitable setting for a

---

[1] In view of its ruinous condition, and of its being 'much in disgrace and out of custom', this rental indicates the important size of the property. This is further shown by its frontage, which appears to have measured 107½ feet.

new professional theatre in Whitechapel to follow up the success of the Theatre. There was apparently no question of partnership with Burbage in the new venture, though the two men were still on good terms, with Burbage backing some of Brayne's bonds arising out of his affairs at the George Inn.

The crucial statement upon Brayne's intentions comes in a Chancery suit brought by Miles against Bestney, from which we learn that when Brayne took the lease of the George from Field he did so 'hoping that he might do some good upon it, intending to build a playhouse therein'.[1] The statement is quite explicit, and its precise wording is significant. The 'inn' is not the 'playhouse'. The 'playhouse' is to be built within the inn, that is, in its yard. The theatre, in fact, is a structure within the precincts of the inn, providing new buildings necessary for its purposes—stage, tiring room, and stands for spectators. We can hardly doubt that this was the pattern for Brayne's earlier Red Lion Theatre, and that the Boar's Head Theatre was designed on this pattern, without any use of the existing buildings of the inn as part of its framework either for stage or for accommodation for spectators.

Probably Brayne set his project afoot at once. This is suggested by records of two of his creditors for work done at the George and left unpaid by him. One of the chief creditors was Noble, a carpenter, as was Sylvester in 1567 at the Red Lion. A second creditor was William Heron, who was a Sergeant Painter to the Queen. We may not unreasonably find grounds in his profession for his association with Brayne. Painters played a large part in the preparation of pageants for the City and the great Guild Companies, and also in providing properties and background cloths for the professional theatre. Heron may well be described in fact as a scenic artist among other things. It is to be recalled that Randolph Maye of Shoreditch was 'a servant in the house called the Theatre' in 1581–2, as Wallace records, and was a painter by trade.[2]

---

[1] C24/314/85; deposition of George Ceeley, gentleman, of Whitechapel, aged sixty-two, in 1605. Bestney, as Field's heir, was the holder of the 'grand lease' from the Manor, and Miles was seeking a renewal of Brayne's lease, which expired in 1605.

[2] C. W. Wallace, 'The First London Theatre', in *Nebraska University Studies*, XII, 1913, p. 240.

The vicissitudes and uncertainties of the theatre-world are notorious. And never was a project more ill-fated than Brayne's proposed George Theatre in Whitechapel. We may say with great assurance that this is the only occasion in history when an earthquake wrecked a theatre before it was built. The year 1580 was disastrous for the stage in London. The unceasing campaign of its enemies was fortified by unexpected and potent ammunition three months after Brayne sealed his lease of the George. On 6 April an earthquake struck fear into men's minds in England and France. In May, Queen Elizabeth sponsored a relief fund, by letters to selected gentlemen in the shires, for the sorely stricken Protestants of Montpellier in France, where especially heavy damage was wrought. 'God's merciful warning by the late earthquake', she wrote, was an extraordinary admonition to England to act with true Christian compassion for the calamity of the afflicted, and so to ward off impending disasters nearer home.[1] It was interpreted in England as a clear sign from Heaven, the dreadful, inarticulate anger of God condemning play-acting, the great sin of London which drew men away from divine service to haunts of iniquity. So the Lord Mayor of London, Sir Nicholas Woodrofe, had already written to the Lord Chancellor on 12 April:

> the players of plays, which are used at the Theatre and other such places, and tumblers, and such like, are a very superfluous sort of men, and of such faculty as the laws have disallowed, and their exercise of those plays is a great hindrance of the service of God, who hath with his mighty hand so lately admonished us of our earnest repentance.[2]

It was unfortunate that both Brayne and Burbage had recently been indicted at the Middlesex Sessions as being responsible for great affrays, assaults, insurrections, and other crimes and enormities arising out of gatherings to see plays at the Theatre on 21 February and other days. Further disorders had occurred a few days before the Lord Mayor's letter.[3] There was evidently reason for the wrath of Heaven.

[1] State Papers Domestic Elizabeth I, CXXXVIII, 37.
[2] Chambers, *The Elizabethan Stage*, IV, 279.
[3] Ibid., IV, pp. 278–9.

Certainly the civic authorities of London exaggerated the pretext which the earthquake gave them to redouble their attack upon the theatre, as might appear from a later repercussion of these events in the publication in 1593 of *A Very Profitable Sermon Entitled 'Morie-mini' Preached before her Majesty at the Court about 14 Years Since.* In this sermon the unknown preacher referred to 'the late earthquake' which, he said, 'did so little damage'.[1] It might seem that the celestial warning was directed rather to Montpellier than to London. But the incident left a lasting impression upon the memories of ordinary Englishmen, for whom it took its place as one of those milestones in history by which they reckoned events of more personal import, rather than by dates or regnal years. So the earthquake joined Flodden Field, the return of King Henry from Boulogne, the execution of the Duke of Buckingham, the arrival of Anne of Cleves, the loss of Calais, the Great Windy Thursday, and other events which loomed so large in retrospect as to be epoch-making. As late as in 1597 a certain John Parnell, testifying to the misdeeds of a French thief in London, fixed the date of his recollections by reference to 'the great earthquake some 18 or 19 years ago', adding precisely that this was on Wednesday in Easter week in that year, as indeed it was.[2]

It might well seem impious to go searching for another earthquake haunting the mind of Shakespeare's Nurse in *Romeo and Juliet*, as projected from the poet's mind: "Tis since the earthquake now eleven years' (I.3.23). The reckoning is precise and leads to the dating of the play in 1591. There can be no question of a topical allusion inserted at a later date by dramatist or gagging actor. No other earthquake can rival the notoriety of the 1580 earthquake. The only defence lies in a denial of the evidence as evidential, in the interests of a fixed idea that Shakespeare's career as a dramatist began at the later date generally accepted. In 1591 he was, after all, twenty-seven years of age. It is perhaps only an odd coincidence that in August 1591 the Queen paid a week's visit to Viscount Montague at Cowdray Park in Sussex, and that in the play the hero Romeo is a Montagu.

---

[1] *A Very Profitable Sermon Entitled 'Moriemini' . . .*, printed by J. Wolf, 1593 (S.T.C. 1034).
[2] C24/258/71. It is recorded also by Gabriel Harvey in *Three Proper Letters* (1580).

The earthquake, at any rate, was used, whether as a pretext or in genuine interpretation of a heavenly portent, as a weapon in the war against the stage, which was stricken as a whole with an inhibition of playing everywhere throughout this year. Brayne suffered also a more particular blast of the general storm, as Mr Ceeley[1] further reported in his evidence, 'being afterwards prohibited to proceed with his playhouse, he bestowed no great matter upon it, but passed his interest over to [Miles]'. On 31 July 1580, in fact, Brayne completed negotiations with Robert Miles, an Essex man from Chigwell, and a freeman of the Goldsmiths' Company, and assigned to him a half-share in his lease of the property. There was ample time between Brayne's acquisition of the lease in January and the disconcerting events of April and May for him to make some beginning on the work of building his proposed theatre and to incur debts for structures the value of which was destroyed at a blow, along with the hopes that had led him to invest in the property. His main anxiety was now to reduce his commitments in an investment that had lost all purpose for him. There is no evidence of any consideration received from Miles in return for the assignment, nor is it probable that the agreement made any demand of this nature, whatever Miles alleged at a later date. The terms of the agreement are intelligible enough. Miles received a half share in the lease, and in return undertook to pay half the rental of £30 and half the cost of expenditure upon the improvement of the property, thus relieving Brayne of half the financial burden imposed on him by his unhappy speculation, and offering the possibility of some return from such alternative development of the premises as might be devised by Miles.

According to Brayne's widow Margaret, Miles was an old friend of Brayne whom he loved well, and whom he provided with lodging in the George for himself, his wife and children as soon as he entered into possession, 'in the poor and low estate that [Miles] was lately fallen into'. He was to work for Brayne in the inn, and pay off his own debts. For Miles the prohibition of the projected theatre came as a boon, changing him from Brayne's servant to his partner. It is plain enough that he was financially a man of straw, and his principal

[1] See p. 14 n.

activities were raising capital by loans upon the property, including a mortgage of £60 within a year, as appears from his own statements in suits which escaped the attention of Wallace. By 1584 Brayne was in dire straits. He had in fact paid the whole rent for the property and had provided £240 for current expenditure in addition to the cost of redeeming loans and mortgages upon the George. Miles had gradually taken affairs into his own hands, and upon the death of Brayne in 1586 was able to claim the whole property as his own and to deny any interest of Brayne's widow in this part of Brayne's estate.[1]

In the crowded calendar of Miles's litigation, it appears that some attempt was at first made to continue the George as an inn, despite its disrepair. But the building was soon remodelled and adapted to provide a group of tenements rented to occupiers. And the adjacent garden grounds and Mill House were let for the development of malodorous industries, the manufacture of vinegar and of soap. The great theatre of Brayne's concept was drowned in a noisome sea of slum-property and of such factories as for centuries continued to offend the nostrils of the East End of London.

Brayne was 'but a plain and simple man', as reported by John Allen, an innkeeper of St Botolph's,[2] the last person to be able to cope with the unscrupulous and grasping Miles, who got him and his widow alike into his clutches, and who involved Mrs Brayne in a dispute with her brother-in-law James Burbage, resulting in costly litigation from which only Miles, the mainspring of the action, could possibly profit. Brayne died a ruined man in 1586. Mrs Brayne died in 1593, and Miles's annexation of the family assets was completed under the terms of her will, bequeathing to him her share in the profits of the Theatre, the fruits of Brayne's partnership with Burbage. If ever a will reeked of undue influence, it was Margaret Brayne's, with Miles as its executor and beyond doubt the dictator of its provisions.[3] When we consider

---

[1] The property did not, of course, figure in Brayne's will, which was drawn up in 1578, two years before he acquired the lease. See Commissary Court of London, Register 1585–92 (Guildhall Library), p. 29.

[2] C. W. Wallace, 'The First London Theatre', in *Nebraska University Studies*, XII, 1913, p. 101.

[3] Commissary Court of London, Register 1592–7 (Guildhall Library), p. 26; see Wallace, p. 153, in whose transcript for 'any saige [sic] comynge' read 'any waye comynge'.

the whole sum of circumstances which led Burbage and his associates to abandon the Theatre in Shoreditch and to rebuild it as the Globe on Bankside, we should not leave out of account the nullification of Miles's piracy of Brayne's share in the profits of the Theatre, which now ceased to exist.

Richard and Cuthbert Burbage certainly did less than justice to the share of their father's partner in the founding of the London Theatre. Brayne was the first in the field as financier of the Red Lion for the use of Burbage's company, and for nearly twenty years devoted his means and his energies to the provision of further theatres in London. His venture upon the George Inn was disastrous, and with the intrusion of Miles into his affairs, he got plainly out of his depth. But it is clear that he was absorbingly interested throughout in the development of the exciting new world of the professional stage and drama. And even his abortive George Theatre pointed the way to a later venture of a similar nature in the same populous suburb of London, the Boar's Head in Whitechapel. We can hardly exaggerate the significance of the fact that the erection of permanent structures for theatrical purposes in inn-yards occurred or was proposed four or possibly five times over a period covering Elizabeth's reign, in 1557 possibly at the Boar's Head, in 1567 at the Red Lion, in 1580 at the George, in 1594 at the Boar's Head again, and in 1605 at the Red Bull, while from 1576 onwards the construction of theatres built from the ground ran a parallel course in the development of stage and drama.

Chapter III

The Boar's Head Inn

Location and Early History

What little was known when Chambers wrote his account of the Boar's Head Inn[1] may be briefly recapitulated. The performance of 'a lewd play' entitled *A Sackful of News* is recorded on 5 September 1557 at the Boar's Head without Aldgate. Towards the end of Elizabeth's reign, on 31 March 1602, the Privy Council exhorted the Lord Mayor to permit the use of the Boar's Head by the combined company of Oxford and Worcester, with the stipulation that they should be tied to that one house. The Boar's Head was chosen, 'because we are informed the house called the Boar's Head is the place they have especially used and do best like of' (Chambers, IV, 335). An undated draft of a licence for this company, described as the Queen's Men, which places it after 1603, authorises them to act 'within their now usual housen, called the Curtain and the Boar's Head, within our County of Middlesex, [or] as in any other play house not used by others' (Chambers, II, 230). In 1608 the Duke of York's Men are described as 'the Prince's players of the White Chapel, London', and J. Q. Adams interpreted this as a further reference to the Boar's Head.[2] Finally, Joan Alleyn's letter to her husband Edward Alleyn, then on tour in the provinces, records the news, in October 1603, that 'Browne of the Boar's Head is dead, and died very poor'.[3] Chambers finds it

[1] Chambers, *The Elizabethan Stage*, II, pp. 443-5.
[2] See Chambers, op. cit., II, pp. 242, 444. Their leader was John Garland, 'of the Old Ford', Whitechapel: see Chambers, op cit., II, p. 241.
[3] *Henslowe's Diary*, ed. R. A. Foakes and R. T. Rickert, 1961, p. 297.

impossible to identify this 'Browne', but the new evidence certifies that it was in fact Robert Browne, once leader of Worcester's Men. This was the meagre extent of our previous knowledge.

The Boar's Head Inn, however, emerges again in documentary records, at a long interval after the reference to the performance there under Queen Mary in 1557, as the property in 1594 of Jane Poley, the widow of Edmund Poley, and of their son Henry Poley, and again in use as a theatre.

The earliest recorded use of the Boar's Head as a theatre, in 1557, links it unexpectedly with the More circle. The Lord of the Manor of Stepney was then Thomas Lord Wentworth, and William Roper, Sir Thomas More's son-in-law, was Steward of the Manor under Wentworth, as Roper himself twice testifies in Chancery depositions of 1562–3.[1] The extant records of Stepney Manor date only from 1652, but the new evidence now under consideration makes it certain that the Boar's Head, in 1594 as in 1557, was held from the Manor of Stepney or Stebenheath. Roper was succeeded as Steward by one Stewkley at some date after 1563, and Stewkley by Edmund Poley in 1573. Poley was landlord of the Boar's Head as well as Steward of the Manor, as we shall see. The Manor was an appanage of the Bishopric of London. Bishop Tunstall, More's friend, had granted it, along with the Manor of Hackney, to Giles Heron, who married Cecily More in 1525. Upon Heron's attainder and execution in 1551 under Edward VI, Ridley, then Bishop of London, was authorised to grant both Manors to Wentworth.[2] We may well consider with some astonishment the spectacle of William Roper attending upon the new Lord of the Manor at Shacklewell House, the mansion for so long of his brother-in-law Giles Heron and of Cecily, sister of his wife Margaret More. It is a disconcerting spectacle, and it confirms other evidence of Roper's opportunism which brought him safely out of dangerous times with increased prosperity. This evidence has its bearing upon the debated question of the location of the Boar's Head Inn.

There need be no doubt, in fact, that the Boar's Head Inn without

---

[1] C24/55/Henshaw; C24/56/Barnes. Aged sixty-four on 14 May 4 Eliz. 1562; aged sixty-four on 24 February 5 Eliz. 1563; 'steward of the Manor of Stepney'.

[2] *Patent Rolls Edward VI*, IV (1926), 15 December 1551, p. 50. Ridley himself lived at the Bishopric's Manor of Fulham, hard by More's former estate in Chelsea.

Aldgate used as a theatre in 1557 was the same Boar's Head in White-chapel on record as a theatre used by the company of Worcester's Men and by the same company when they became Queen Anne's Men, in 1602–3. The site of the Boar's Head Theatre is commemorated in the street-name, Boar's Head Yard, leading off Whitechapel Street on its north side between Middlesex Street and Goulston Street. So J. Q. Adams assumes;[1] Chambers, however, rejects these identifications.[2]

In his view, the 'inn without Aldgate' which in 1557 was the scene of the offensive *A Sackful of News* lay in the extra-mural Portsoken Ward, between Aldgate and the bars limiting the liberties of the City at Hog Lane. It was thus within the jurisdiction of the City, which had put an end in 1596 to the licensing of play-houses, so it could not have been used as a theatre after that year. He justly points out that a letter from the Privy Council on 31 March 1602 recommends to the Lord Mayor the allowance of Oxford's and Worcester's Men at the Boar's Head. Though a draft patent for the Curtain and the Boar's Head describes both as 'within our County of Middlesex', he argues that both the inn without Aldgate of 1557 and Boar's Head Yard were within the liberties of the City. Whitechapel proper, he maintains, lies eastwards outside the liberties, as against Ogilby's and Rocque's maps of 1677 and 1746. Chambers concludes that the site of the Boar's Head Theatre cannot be identified with that of the Aldgate inn of 1557 or with Boar's Head Yard, or with the theatre used by the Duke of York's Men in 1608 when they are described as 'the Prince's Players of Whitechapel', and that it was not a converted inn at all, but may have merely borrowed its name from the Blue Boar Inn which is shown in Aldgate High Street in Ogilby's map of 1677. We are left with the implicit alternative that the Boar's Head must have been a building erected in Whitechapel solely for use as a theatre, a con-clusion which Chambers, intelligibly, evades.

It is, however, now quite certain, in the first place, that the Boar's Head Theatre of 1602 was an inn converted to theatrical purposes. It is consistently referred to in both Chancery and Star Chamber docu-ments as an inn, and its situation is defined:

[1] *Shakespearean Playhouses*, 1917, p. 17.
[2] *The Elizabethan Stage*, II, pp. 443–4.

> one customary and copyhold messuage tenement and inn commonly called the Boar's Head on the north side of Whitechapel Street in the parish of Saint Mary Matfellon alias Whitechapel in the County of Middlesex.

> one messuage or inn called the Boar's Head set and lying in White Chapel Street near London.

> the tenements or inn called the Boar's Head without Aldgate, London.

The evidence is unanimous that it was an inn, situated in the parish of Whitechapel or, in its alternative name, the parish of St Mary Matfellon, which was variously described as in Middlesex, near London, or without Aldgate, London. In Chancery decrees it is mostly referred to simply as 'the inn called the Boar's Head'. It is perhaps not without significance that in one such decree an attachment was directed for execution to the Sheriff of London, not of Middlesex, in a suit relating to the Boar's Head. But it is apparent in many ways that the administrative entities of Middlesex and extramural London were ill-defined in the general mind. It is clear also that the writ of London and its Lord Mayor ran by no means without question, and frequently failed to be enforced. It was hampered and even overruled by the superior authority of the Privy Council, and strongly influenced by the interests of such great nobles as the Earl of Derby or Worcester.

The Court and the parish alike profited from the activities of the theatre. We learn of the considerable expenditure required to meet the vested interests of the Master of the Revels, and to maintain Court influence in favour of any particular theatre. The parish imposed, or received, regular weekly contributions for the poor. There was an element of confusion apparent in the remains of an older, feudal world which preserved some of the rights of the Liberty or Manor of Stepney as against those of the Liberties of London. The Boar's Head Inn was held in customary or copyhold tenure from Thomas, Lord Wentworth, Lord of that Manor. There can be no doubt about this question of title, a constant element in descriptions of the property. Indeed, about Christmas 1602 the 'bailiffs of the liberty of Stebenheath' took possession of the Boar's Head on behalf of Oliver Wood-lif.[1] Finally, it would seem clear that Boar's Head Yard on the north of Whitechapel Street is in fact outside the limits of Portsoken Ward, just east of the bars, according to contemporary maps of the area. There is every reason for identifying the Boar's Head of 1602–3 with the Boar's Head, an Aldgate inn, of 1557, and for accepting Boar's Head Yard as recording its situation in Whitechapel.

In the absence of records of Stepney Manor before 1652, the authentic history of the Boar's Head Inn begins with the tenure of the inn from the Manor by its Steward, Edmund Poley, recorded in the law-suits now under consideration. Edmund Poley[2] was a lawyer, giving his address as Gray's Inn on 22 June 1588. In 1582 he is described as 'gentleman, of Whitechapel' in a Chancery suit in which he was a plaintiff.[3] From this suit we learn that he was brother-in-law to John Grove, an attorney of the Common Pleas, and to John Squier, an innholder in High Holborn. The suit has a special interest as illustrating the growing complexity of the law in Elizabethan days. It was an appeal in Chancery against a judgment of the Court of the Liberty of the Tower of London, a court unknown to legal history and without extant records. A reputable witness describes it as 'newly devised' in 1578 by the then Lieutenant of the Tower and the Steward of the Liberty, one Berkeley. Poley was involved as a surety for Grove, and emerges as a man who honoured his word, and left 'not one groat or denier' unpaid upon his bonds. His family history from 1562 onwards is recorded in the Registers of Whitechapel Parish,[4] beginning with the marriage on 14 January 1562 of 'Edmund Powlie and Jane Tranfeld'. The burial of 'John Trunpheild' on 11 November 1561 records the death of the first husband of Poley's wife Jane, following upon the baptism of 'Anne Tranfeild' on 5 July in the same

---

[1] C24/304/27; 1603.

[2] I use the spelling 'Poley' in preference to 'Pooley' in deference to the spelling of his own name in the signature 'Edmund Poley' in a Chancery deposition of 1588 (C24/201/Glascock *v* Goodman). He does not, unfortunately, give his age in the usual way in the preliminaries to his evidence.

[3] C24/157/Poley and Squier *v* Robert Harrison and Mary Bedingfield.

[4] Preserved on deposit in the Record Room of London County Council at County Hall, in a large bound volume on vellum and remarkably well kept. The record is complete from 1558 onwards.

year.[1] Two months after her husband's death Jane was married to Poley. A son Henry was baptised on 20 December 1562, a second son John on 28 October 1565, and a daughter Elizabeth on 13 December 1566. On 11 August 1587 the burial of 'Edmund Pooly' is recorded, but he was certainly alive in June 1588, though dead before 1591.[2]

In 1573, according to Poley's own evidence, he became Steward of the Manor of Stepney by the appointment of Thomas, Lord Wentworth.[3] In this capacity, he became involved in the long debate between the Lord of the Manor and his copyhold tenants who sought to obtain conditions of tenancy more in keeping with ordinary freeholds than with the feudal restrictions of manorial tenures. An agreement was arrived at, and a new system of manorial customs was drawn up. It was printed without indication of printer, apparently for distribution to copyholders concerned, and is dated 10 November 1587.[4] Lord Wentworth received from them £3,000, and entered into bonds to assure his implementation of the agreement, ultimately by Act of Parliament. A further payment of £3,500 in 1617 was followed by an agreed decree enrolled in Chancery and by a private Act four years later. It is evident that Poley had a large part to play in the first agreement of 1587. His name came first in the list of five witnesses to this document. His heirs now had power to make leases of their copyhold property without licence from the Manor for periods not exceeding thirty-one years, along with other freedoms from manorial control. The Boar's Head Inn was such a property.

Like many another Elizabethan woman of property, Edmund's widow Jane Poley was illiterate, as appears from her will,[5] to which she affixed her mark in 1601. It appears further from her will that she was a Berkshire woman, born at White Walton, and we might conclude that the copyhold of the Boar's Head came to her through her marriage with John Transfeld. But when the property was leased to a theatrical speculator in 1594 it was owned by Mrs Poley and her

[1] 'John Transefeld' is identified as Jane's first husband in C24/225/58.
[2] See pp. 26–7 n.
[3] C24/201/Glascock *v* Goodman.
[4] The earliest surviving edition (S.T.C. 23252) is conjecturally dated 1610. It is reprinted in several later published books upon the *Customs of the Manors of Stepney and Hackney.*
[5] P. C. C. Woodhall 47, dated 16 April and proved on 8 July 1601.

eldest son Henry by Edmund Poley, not by Mrs Poley and her daughter Anne by Transfeld. It might seem most probable that Poley's Stewardship of the Manor went with his ownership of the copyhold of the Boar's Head, which descended to his widow and his eldest son upon his death before 1591. Upon Henry's death before 1601 it may have come into the possession of his second son, Sir John Poley,[1] subject to Jane's life-interest. Henry is not mentioned in Jane's will, nor any child of his, and all her landed property is left to Sir John, her sole executor. 'A great garden' in Whitechapel was bought by Poley in 1572, and in 1591 was owned jointly by Jane and Henry, after Edmund's death.[2] Jane's will names it as 'Woodlands in Whitechapel, abutting on North hoglane', and the grand lease is bequeathed to Sir John, along with other leases and rents.

Mrs Poley was clearly a woman of means, with a wealth of jewellery and fine clothes, able to leave £40 to one needy daughter Frances with four children and to remember with considerable bequests other relatives, her old servants, a group of godchildren, and the poor of Whitechapel and of White Walton. She was a leading member of a numerous clan in Whitechapel. They are not easy to disentangle.[3] Apparently Edmund had sisters married to John Grove and John Squier, and Jane had sisters Mrs White and Mrs Trigge. Her daughter Anne Transfeld married Henry Gibbs on 8 September 1586 at the age of twenty-five. By Poley, Jane had six children: Henry, John, Elizabeth (Mrs Miller), Frances (Mrs Wybard), and Isobel and Ralph who both died at an early age in 1577. Mrs Poley certainly showed some attachment to the Boar's Head. It may be that she and Edmund made it their residence, with Richard Samwell as manager of the inn, and with Edmund maintaining his lawyer's office in Gray's Inn. Certainly Mrs Poley lived in the inn from 1594 onwards, with rooms reserved for her own use. She may have taken up a residence so convenient for a wealthy widow upon the death of Edmund before 1591.[4] She died there in 1601.

---

[1] Knighted by Essex at Dublin in 1599, at the age of thirty-three.
[2] C24/225/58. It was in proximity to the Boar's Head.
[3] C24/157 Poley *v* Harrison; Mrs Poley's will; Whitechapel Parish Registers.
[4] A disconcerting entry in the Parish Register records the burial of 'Edmund Poley' on 11 August 1587. Poley, however, gave evidence in Chancery in June 1588. The

On 28 November 1594 Jane and Henry Poley leased the Boar's Head Inn to Oliver Woodlif and his wife Susan for twenty-one years, the lease to begin from the following Lady Day, 25 March 1595, and to run to 24 March 1616. Before the agreement of 1587 negotiated by Edmund Poley, such a lease required a preliminary licence from the Lord of the Manor, and even Poley as Steward might have hesitated to make a case for the grant of a licence, where the lessee's intention was to develop the inn as a theatre. Lord Wentworth, in his capacity as a Middlesex Justice, was closely associated with the war waged by the City and the Privy Council upon the theatre. In 1577 he was especially charged to extend to playing in Middlesex outside the Liberties of the City the same embargo which the Lord Mayor had imposed within the City. In 1578 he attended a conference with the Lord Mayor upon the same subject, and in 1580 was again charged to restrain playing in Middlesex.[1] It was doubtless he who had an interdict laid upon Brayne's proposed theatre in the George Inn in Whitechapel. The evidence is clear that the Boar's Head was already in use as a theatre. But such a lease, with such a purpose, would have been an open challenge both to the Lord of the Manor and to the Lord Mayor by its close proximity to the City. The situation had changed, however, in 1594. Poley had died before 1591, and a new Lord ruled the Manor of Stepney. Mrs Poley was a free agent, as her husband was not, and she had every reason to seek a regular income from the property, without the responsibilities of being its landlord.

The lease to the Woodlifs included the whole of the inn and its garden and back-yard. According to Woodlif's own account of the transaction, it provided for payment of a rent of £40, with a covenant whereby he undertook to expend £100 within seven years 'in building of the larder, the larder parlour, the well parlour, the coal house, the oat loft, the tiring house and stage'.[2] Woodlif entered into a bond of

copying on vellum, under an order of 1598, of original paper Registers often led to error on the part of the incumbent or his scribe. It may be that Poley's death was recorded in this vellum copy under the wrong year, possibly instead of 1588. He was certainly dead before 1591, the date of the suit concerning the 'great garden'. The scribe of these Registers signs his copy as 'Anthony Caulnay' and dates it 1599, in the '29th year of Richard Gardener parson'.

[1] Chambers, op. cit., IV, pp. 276–7, 280.
[2] Requests 2/466, Part Two.

£300 to perform this work, and failure to complete it entailed for-
feiture of his lease. Mrs Poley clearly attached importance to the
maintenance and improvement of the structure of the inn. It was,
after all, her home. All accounts agree that certain rooms were reserved
from the lease for Mrs Poley's own residence, doubtless under a
further covenant. These consisted of two rooms on the first floor of
the inn in the west wing of the yard, and they are sometimes referred
to as her 'house'. She continued to enjoy the right to draw water from
the pump in the yard. Woodlif himself, upon completion of the lease,
occupied for his own use and his wife's a parlour and chambers over
the entrance gate and adjacent to it. It is clear from his statement that
Richard Samwell was landlord of the inn as the Poleys' employee and
that he continued to manage it under Woodlif until 1598, when
Woodlif assigned the inn-premises to him. Samwell describes himself
as a 'yeoman' without indication of any trade, as often with innkeepers. He had a married son Richard who shared with him the
management of the inn. Samwell and his family were also resident in
the inn, its accommodation being thus charged with three suites of
chambers for permanent occupation. Woodlif describes himself as a
haberdasher by trade. He travelled abroad on his business, probably
as an importer of French silk goods. He occupied a shop in the Royal
Exchange in 1597,[1] and is not known otherwise as having any connection with the theatre.

The accommodation of the Boar's Head Inn was on a large scale,
with no fewer than thirteen chambers on the first floor, providing
hospitality if necessary to some twenty guests in days when chambers
and beds were frequently shared, not necessarily by married couples or
friends only. It can hardly be doubted that when the inn was leased
to Woodlif by the Poley's it afforded ample provision for its normal
business, standing as it did on the main road leading eastward into
Middlesex and Essex. There are clear indications, moreover, that the
Whitechapel district was in rapid process of development from the
'hamlet' of manorial records into a London suburb. In 1572, the
Poleys leased to Henry Browne, a clothmaker, a 'great garden' in
Whitechapel Parish for twenty-one years, at a rental of £36 a year.

[1] C24/258/6 and 58.

It had been owned by John and Jane Transfeld before Jane married Edmund Poley. Browne developed in this garden-area seven small properties, each with a house and a garden, fenced off from one another, the whole area permitting of thirty such tenements.[1] The George Inn, again, falling into desuetude as an inn, was converted to residential and industrial uses. Parish records reflect visibly the rapidly growing population of the district,[2] and the variety of occupations pursued there may be seen in Chancery records of Whitechapel affairs, glovers, tailors, butchers, clothworkers, matmakers, soapmakers, cross-bow makers, and armourers. There was a strong element of Flemish immigrants. And the district attracted floating vagrants, some of Irish origin. Certainly it might seem that the Boar's Head Inn offered opportunity for the provision of theatrical entertainment beyond the needs of transient traffic along a main artery, to supply the population of Whitechapel no less than that of the neighbouring City of London. It is fortunate that we have exceptionally full details of the structure which served the purposes of the Boar's Head Theatre.

Structure and Accommodation of the Inn

A full description of the accommodation contained in the inn-buildings is available in several accounts agreeing with and supplementing each other. The entrance to the inn, on the north of Whitechapel Street, led into a great yard surrounded by two-storied buildings and running from south to north, with its exit at its north end, outside of which a garden, or back-yard, beyond the limits of the inn itself, formed part of the property. The information given supplies most of the material necessary for plans showing the layout of the structure on the ground floor and on the first floor. The general scheme of the layout in certain important respects corresponds closely with the constant pattern that appears in such Elizabethan inns as survived to be recorded for later study, as at Southwell and at

[1] C24/225/58. Maggs v Poley. Michaelmas 33/34 Eliz. 1581.
[2] In the plague epidemic of 1563 some 300 burials are recorded from July to November. By 1603, Professor F. P. Wilson told me, the deaths in one year from plague exceeded 1,350 in the parish.

Aylesbury, a pattern that is intelligible and logical for the innkeeper and his customers.

There is unfortunately no indication of the measurements in length or width of the buildings or of the yards, or of the area occupied. Some clue might perhaps be sought in the known measurements of the Fortune Theatre, a building 80 feet square surrounding a yard 55 feet square, with a stage 43 feet wide by $27\frac{1}{2}$ feet deep.[1] Assuming the need for sufficient space in the Boar's Head yard, the area enclosed by its permanent buildings, for galleries and stage on the model of the Fortune, and providing for those permanent buildings within the whole rectangle of the inn, we arrive at a conjectural rectangle of 105 feet in width and 120 feet in length. This would permit of a theatre-square of 90 feet by 75 feet inside the yard, with galleries, stage, and open space of dimensions approximately those of the Fortune.

Some guide might be sought further in a parallel with the George Inn, also in Whitechapel. There the garden behind the inn, part of its whole rectangle, was $107\frac{1}{2}$ feet in width,[2] suggesting a similar width for its yard and for that of the Boar's Head, whatever its length. Presumably the length would be somewhat greater, and indeed the known buildings require it. A rectangle of 105 feet by 120 feet appears to satisfy the requirements of the inn-buildings and of the theatre constructed in its yard. The constant repetition of the phrase 'great yard' in relation to the Boar's Head suggests indeed an even more spacious area within its buildings. Francis Langley describes it as 'the great Court'.

The entrance-gate led through a solid structure into the yard. On its right hand was a 'drinking room' or tavern-room, and on the left the hall or main dining-room. These two principal rooms, with the entrance-structure, formed the façade of the inn towards Whitechapel Street, and led on the ground floor into suites of rooms occupying the two wings of connecting buildings on either side of the rectangular yard. On its west wing the hall was linked with a dining-parlour and beyond it the kitchen. On its east wing the tavern-room was adjoined

---

[1] The builder's contract for the Fortune is reproduced by Chambers in *The Elizabethan Stage*, II, pp. 436–9.

[2] See Chapter II above.

by a suite of three parlours and a cellar-room beyond them. The main cellar was a basement room underneath part of the hall, and was the only structure under the yard level. Provision was thus made both for general eating and drinking, and for private or select parties in the parlours.

The rest of the ground floor was devoted to provision for the horses of the inn's customers. On the west wing, next to the kitchen, was the ostlery-room with a back room behind it, and then a main stable, and opposite these rooms, on the east wing, three further stables. There was thus provision for private stables as for private parlours, as well as a general stable. The yard was closed at its north end by a barn with an opening for the exit gate, and with a hay-loft over its eastern half. The exit-gate gave on to a garden or back-yard behind the inn, part of which had been let since about 1580 to Roger and Alice Saunders of Whitechapel.[1] Mrs Saunders describes her holding as a 'garden plot' belonging to the Boar's Head Inn. But the back-yard provided also a place of deposit for dung from the inn and for the flow from the inn's primitive drainage system of channels and gutters. The privy which is cited among the buildings is not located, but was probably situated at the north end of the yard, near to the stables and to the back-yard, perhaps between the third stable and the barn. There was a well with a pump in the yard to serve all purposes. Woodlif refers to 'the well parlour' and to 'the larder parlour'. The larder would certainly be in close relation to the kitchen, and 'the larder parlour' may be identified with the dining-parlour next to the kitchen in the west wing, in which there was no other parlour on the ground floor. 'The well parlour' must therefore have been one of the three drinking-parlours in the east wing of the inn. The well and pump were thus located in the yard outside one of these parlours, opposite the kitchen across the yard, conveniently for the tavern, if not for the kitchen or for the chambers in the west wing. The 'coal house' of which mention is made must surely have been in close relation with the kitchen, perhaps with an external opening for delivery.

The upper storey of the inn, on both wings, was almost entirely composed of chambers opening upon galleries running round the

[1] Roger evidently still held it in 1601, when he witnessed Mrs Poley's will.

yard on all sides except the north. The whole of the east wing was occupied by seven chambers, all seven opening upon one gallery, and beyond them the loft of the barn at the end of the yard, east of the exit gate. This suggests clearly the architectural unity of the building on both floors. The arrangement of the west wing leads to a different conclusion. There the upper floor of the entrance gate was occupied by one parlour, known as the 'upper parlour' or the 'hither parlour', that of the hall by two chambers, and that of the kitchen by one chamber. Presumably these rooms occupied between them the area of the dining-parlour as well as the hall and kitchen. The area of the ostlery provided a loft on the first floor, which is probably that referred to by Woodlif as 'the oat loft'. The wing then continued beyond the ostlery with the two chambers over the main stable retained by Mrs Poley for her own residence, at the north end of this west wing of the yard. The western half of the barn was apparently a one-storey building, though provided with a loft on the east side of the exit gate.

There is some insistence upon the unity of structure of hall, parlour and kitchen 'on one floor', which suggests a break between the kitchen and the ostlery on the ground floor, possibly with a passage between them and a door in the west wall of the yard. This is supported by the break in the provision of chambers on the first floor to allow for the loft over the ostlery. The gallery on the west side may of course have been continuous, the normal access to a loft being by ladder and trapdoor, with the wall of the loft blind on the gallery-side. But Mrs Poley's selection of rooms, referred to sometimes as her 'house', may have been determined by a desire for privacy and isolation from the general movement of the inn. They probably had a separate and private gallery. The passage, with a separate gate to close it, may have served as a kind of 'tradesmen's entrance' for supplies, and possibly for horses on their way to the stables. It may also have been an alternative entrance for actors and others, when the main gate of entry was closed and controlled for performances in the theatre.

No information is available concerning staircases from the yard or ground floor of the inn to the upper storey. We can only depend upon analogies from other recorded inns, and the obvious needs of the structure. It is reasonably certain that all staircases were external, leading from the yard to the galleries which gave access to first-floor rooms. Three such staircases appear to be necessary. Two of them would mount, one on each side of the entrance, to the chambers above. That on the east side of the gate led to the seven chambers there. That on the west side led to Woodlif's quarters over the entrance and hall and to the remaining chambers beyond his. Mrs Poley required a staircase at the north-west corner of the yard to her private rooms. Presumably all three were corner-staircases, to leave the yard freer. A fourth staircase at the north-east corner seems unnecessary. The situation of the staircase obviously might affect the structure of stage, tiring house, and stands for spectators in adapting the inn-yard for theatrical purposes.

It is clear that Samwell, landlord of the inn, was also resident there, with his son Richard, aged sixteen at the date of the lease, and by 1601 a daughter-in-law Winifred, and one grand-child.[1] The most convenient rooms available for their occupation were apparently the two chambers adjacent to Woodlif's parlour and chamber, one over half the hall, and one over the kitchen. If so, the whole of the chamber accommodation in the west wing was taken up by Woodlif, Samwell, and Mrs Poley. We may well have some curiosity about the use of the seven chambers in the east wing, especially when the theatre was in full operation. It is an irresistible temptation to guess that the company of actors occupied these chambers, which could well provide for its leader and sharers. It would certainly be most convenient to have the main part of the company housed on the premises, with tavern and restaurant facilities available, and this might be an attraction for the company contemplating the theatre. This consideration, of course, fortifies the belief that an inn taken over for theatrical purposes was obliged to abandon its function as a provider of lodging, though not as a purveyor of drink and meals, for casual customers. It becomes increasingly intelligible that the leader and manager of a company of actors, Robert Browne, should venture upon the acquisition of the Boar's Head property as a whole, including its catering provisions, its yard and theatre, and its considerable sets of chambers. It seemed to meet all his needs and solve all his problems.

[1] Sara, baptised 24 February 1601 (Whitechapel Parish Register).

Certainly it would be immensely advantageous to have the company resident in the premises of the theatre, not least for all the necessary preparations that form part of the production of a play. Historians of the stage and commentators on the drama have paid scant attention to Elizabethan problems of production and rehearsal in the actual daily practical life of a repertory company. Their attention has been riveted mainly to two aspects of their work, to the physical structure of the stages which conditioned their productions, and to the processes of revision, transcription, and preparation which led from the dramatist's text to the prompt-copy and to the printing of a play. It seems to be generally assumed that Elizabethan plays were only perfunctorily rehearsed. But it is difficult to reconcile this notion with the highly professional quality of the great companies. It was surely impossible to perform a complex, tightly constructed play like *Hamlet*, with its large cast and occasionally crowded stage, without detailed designs of movement, rigidly adhered to, and tested in rehearsal, far beyond any simple 'dress rehearsal' run-through for words. It may be that the leader or manager of a company was the all-important 'producer' of its plays for the most part, and certainly not its leading actor. So Heminges or Condell might 'produce' for Richard Burbage, and Christopher Beeston for Richard Perkins. There is ample evidence that the author of a play too had a considerable say in its production and acting, far beyond modern practice. Shakespeare indeed was probably in a very real sense the producer of his own plays.[1]

The inn-yard theatre perhaps offered difficulties for rehearsals on stage unless access to the yard was inhibited at all times. But the occupation by the actors of the chambers on the east wing would give every facility for the earlier processes of production, reading, casting, cutting, scribal preparation of actors' parts, songs and music, and the like. The theory of a repertory company resident in its own theatre is certainly tempting, and its realisation in the premises of the Boar's Head would be tempting to an Elizabethan company of actors.

There remains the large barn at the north end of the yard. It may

---

[1] See David Klein, 'Did Shakespeare produce his own Plays?', *Modern Language Review*, 57, 1962, pp. 556–60.

have served the company as a work-shop and property-store, and possibly even as a rehearsal-room and meeting-place. No hint is to be found in the documents, however, to give rise to these various conjectures upon the use of the chambers on the east side of the yard or of the barn. The use of the chambers on the west side is authenticated only for the owner's occupation of the parlour over the entrance for Mrs Poley's rooms, and for the fact of Samwell's residence in the inn with his family.

The Inn and Theatre from 1594 to 1599

Woodlif's object in seeking the lease of the Boar's Head Inn from the Poleys was clearly to develop it for the purposes of a public theatre. His interest was apparently purely financial. A haberdasher of London, active in his trade with the Continent, he shows no respect for the acting profession, and refers to Robert Browne as 'a common stage-player' to discredit him in a law-suit. It would seem from the terms of his lease of the inn from the Poleys that his first intention was merely to undertake a modest outlay of £100 as a condition of the grant of the lease, in addition to a rent of £40, and that more ambitious projects were entered upon subsequently.

There is unfortunately little information about the state of the yard in relation to its use as a theatre before Woodlif's lease of 1594 and since the recorded production there of *A Sackful of News* in 1557. But all the evidence suggests a reasonable conclusion that the Boar's Head had continued to be in use as at least an occasional theatre before Woodlif took possession. Woodlif's speculation was hardly likely to be attracted to a Whitechapel inn merely as an inn, in the hope of founding a theatre there at a cost of £100, part of which was to be spent on normal inn buildings. The exact terms of the covenant repay study. Woodlif was bound to expenditure not on 'a tiring house and stage' but on 'the tiring house and stage', along with 'the larder, the larder parlour', and other rooms, all cited surely as already in existence. And £100 would appear to be a meagre allowance for such a programme of building new structures. The covenant was therefore for repairs and improvements of existing structure, as probably with the Red Lion earlier on. It is to be borne in mind, moreover, that this covenant was inserted at the instance of the Poleys, as part of the consideration for the grant of the lease. It can hardly be doubted, therefore, that they were concerned that the stage and tiring house should be maintained by Woodlif, if not because of any interest in plays and playing, then presumably as security for such a continued revenue from the inn as would ensure the regular payment of their rent by Woodlif. It is reasonable to think that the death of Edmund Poley decided his widow to part with control of the inn.

The evidence points clearly to the acquisition by Woodlif of an inn with a theatre in its yard as a going concern open to development. It would seem that this was its condition while Edmund Poley was its landlord, with Richard Samwell as his tenant. There is perhaps further support for this view in the description of the inn as leased by the Poleys to Woodlif which refers to its 'edifices, barns, buildings, stables, yards, ways and passages'.[1] The use of both words, 'edifices' and 'buildings' thus separated, suggests that 'edifices' included such abnormal features as a stage and a tiring house, which appear to have been permanent structures in the yard. The subsequent lease of the inn in 1598 by Woodlif to Samwell, which inventories its accommodation, naturally makes no reference to stage or tiring house in the yard, as the yard was not included in the lease. A later verbal agreement of 1599 between Woodlif and Samwell, however, specifies them, as well as the galleries in the yard. It seems clear that the previous equipment of the yard included a gallery for spectators on the west side of the inn.

Woodlif's contribution to the theatre in the yard was therefore the repair, reconstruction, and enlargement of its existing facilities for plays, in an increasing concentration of the inn and its yard upon the business of a theatre. It is apparent that the occupation of the yard by such structures as stage, tiring house, and galleries or stands would impede at all times the normal business of an inn, especially the movement of carriers' wagons through and out of the yard. It may well be that the Boar's Head, like the George Inn in 1580, was de-

[1] Star Chamber 5, S74/3.

clining in activity and popularity as an inn proper. Certainly, when it was in full use as a theatre, the ordinary affairs of an inn must have come to a stop, except for the provision of food and drink for the patrons of the theatre. Its lessee was given full power to close all gates from eleven in the morning of performances, as indisputable evidence records, in order to restrict entry to paying spectators.

Woodlif's tenure of the Boar's Head began at Lady Day 25 March 1595, when he went into residence there with his wife Susan, occupying a parlour over the entry and probably chambers adjacent.[1] The inn was managed by Samwell for the Poleys, and Woodlif continued to employ him as innkeeper, and also as his agent in the building work projected in the inn yard and executed in part between 1595 and 1598. Woodlif's principal contribution to the facilities of his theatre appears to have been the extension of the gallery for spectators on the west side of the yard, and the addition to it of a second storey. The work was carried out under Samwell's direction during Woodlif's absences on business abroad, and in part was financed by Samwell. More elaborate and complete provision of galleries on all sides of the yard was projected, in consultation between Woodlif and Samwell. But before they were put into execution, Woodlif was driven to reduce his commitments in the Boar's Head. In 1597 he had run into heavy weather with his business and his shop in the Royal Exchange[2] and was in financial difficulties.

On 13 April 1598, Woodlif signed a conveyance to Samwell of all his interest under his lease from the Poleys in respect of the inn and premises other than the yard and its theatre-structures, for eighteen years as from Christmas 1597 to Christmas 1615 at a rental of £40. This arrangement provided for the rent payable by Woodlif to the Poleys on the whole property until a few months before his original lease terminated at Lady Day 1616, and left him as lessee of the yard free of rent. Samwell was now landlord of the inn, and Woodlif landlord of the theatre. There can be little question that the inn-yard was in fact excluded from the transaction, and that Samwell was to enjoy only rights of way through the yard to the inn-premises. The

---

[1] C24/278/71.
[2] C24/258/6 and 58.

garden or back-yard, further, was excluded, except for its use by Samwell as a dung-heap or laystall. There is inconsistency upon these points even in various statements made on behalf of Woodlif at different dates. But it is significant that when these matters came to trial, the indenture of the conveyance was said to be not available for production in court by Woodlif's opponents. The conveyance was testified to, however, by Nicholas Moxsay, servant to Robert Hill, a Notary Public.[1] Moxsay conducted the sealing ceremony in the dining-parlour. He read the document aloud to the interested parties, and they sealed it in his presence. In October 1600, when Moxsay gave evidence, it was in Samwell's possession. The conveyance embodied two covenants to Woodlif's advantage. He and his wife were to retain possession of the parlour and chambers occupied by them in the inn as a residence. Moxsay reports Woodlif's insistence on this during the reading, and Samwell's willing agreement. And Woodlif was to be free to enlarge the gallery on the west side of the yard without respect for the amenities of the inn-premises adjacent to it.

Woodlif was evidently still engaged upon projects for erecting structures serving as a more complete equipment for a theatre. He had complained to Samwell, when inspecting the work done, upon his return from abroad, of its inadequacy to provide the necessary accommodation for spectators. His dissatisfaction suggests a flourishing theatre with an extensive demand for galleries by spectators not content to join the press standing in the open yard. There was clearly justification for further expenditure. A considerable programme was embarked upon, which would surround the yard on all sides with galleries, and enlarge the western gallery and raise it to a second storey, moving the stage to accommodate its extension. The programme was devised in consultation between Woodlif, Samwell, the master-carpenter John Mago and his chief workman, Walter Rodes.[2] Later on, Woodlif denied his part in these plans, and even alleged that he forbade Samwell to proceed with the building and rebuilding of galleries. But he was then concerned to prove that he had not parted with control of the yard and its theatre, and that he was free to

---

[1] C24/278/71.
[2] C24/278/71.

convey his interests in them to another speculator. It was obviously in his interest to increase the accommodation of the western gallery in the yard, of which he shared the profits under a later agreement with Samwell, and there can be no doubt that he financed its extension by Samwell.

The main building programme, however, was in fact financed by Samwell under a further agreement which was not reduced to a formal conveyance and was not secured by bonds. It was entered into by Woodlif and Samwell before witnesses as a verbal lease, doubtless to expedite the work.[1] The evidence for the agreement is beyond cavil in respect both of the making of the agreement and of its terms. Its effect was to transfer to Samwell for the period of his former lease of 1598 the ownership of the yard and its theatre, with the garden, subject to some share in the gallery-receipts, and continuing Woodlif's occupation of his parlour. The grant was made in consideration of Samwell's capital investment in the theatre-buildings, including the cancellation of Woodlif's liabilities to him, and his acceptance of responsibility for running expenses.

The problems of finance and of the design of galleries had led to a conference in the yard itself, in which Woodlif and Samwell had called into consultation John Mago, the master-carpenter, and his workmen, John Marsh and William Hoppdale.

Mago, a man of substance and standing, reports fully upon the terms of the agreement, which was made in his presence at this conference.[2] It was made, as he reports, 'in the great yard of the said inn when the great new galleries were in building in the yard' by Mago himself and his workmen. Both parties, he states, were satisfied with the agreement when it was made, and Samwell carried out duly his

---

[1] A Lease Parole, or verbal lease, was a legitimate and recognised alternative to a written lease. Cowell's *Law Dictionary*, for example, deals with leases under these two forms as of equal validity.

[2] He describes himself on 25 July 1603 as John Mago, of the parish of St Margaret's London, carpenter, aged fifty-six. He was thus born between 26 July 1546 and 25 July 1547. His wife Elizabeth describes herself (C24/350/22) as of Hounsditch in the parish of St Botolph's without Aldgate and of the age of fifty-four at Easter 1610. The William Mago who was a member of Shakespeare's company of actors, and who appears in a minor role in *The Witch of Edmonton* in 1621 and in Massinger's *Believe as you List* in 1631, was probably their son.

side of the bargain. Mago's evidence is borne out by the evidence of Marsh and Hoppdale.[1]

The new agreement affected the respective interests of Woodlif and Samwell in the property as a whole, as an inn and as a theatre. Samwell, as Woodlif's assignee under his lease from the Poleys, controlled the whole of the inn except for a suite of rooms on the first floor next to the exit gate retained by Mrs Poley under her lease to Woodlif, and the parlour hitherto reserved by Woodlif for his own use. The control of the theatre similarly passed to Samwell as Woodlif's assignee, in recognition of his release of Woodlif from responsibility for the capital costs of the erection of new galleries and repairs to stage and tiring houses. Samwell also undertook responsibility for all the miscellaneous expenses involved in the management of a public theatre and the satisfaction of the onerous demands of a variety of authorities, including the Master of the Revels, which weighed heavily upon the entertainment industry.

Woodlif was left with a landlord's half-share in the profits of one of the principal galleries, of which the other half went to the players. This gallery was described by Marsh as having been built by Woodlif himself 'over the stage and at one end of the stage', and Mago agrees that Woodlif's share of the takings was limited to this gallery of his own building. He was thus, reasonably enough, to enjoy a return upon his own capital investment upon accommodation for spectators and upon the stage and tiring house assigned with the yard. For the rest, he was content with the rent of £40 laid down under the 1598 lease to Samwell, which covered his obligations to the Poleys.

The date of this further agreement may be established with reasonable certainty, though there is some conflict of evidence. A Star Chamber Bill of April 1600 reports that it was made in July 1598, the year of the written conveyance of the inn. William Hoppdale, a Whitechapel carpenter who worked for Samwell on the galleries similarly dates the verbal agreement in the same year as the conveyance, at St James's tide (25 July). But in 1601 he dates the conveyance 'about Easter last was two years', that is, in 1599. The most conclusive and circumstantial evidence, which is also the most authoritative, is

---

[1] C24/304/27. July 1603.

that of Richard Samwell the younger, son of Samwell, who was present when the agreement was made in the yard. In Chancery depositions taken in June 1601,[1] he told the Court that it took place 'betwixt midsummer and Bartholomew tide last was twelvemonth viz. about the time that the great training was at Mile End Green, in the time the Earl of Essex was in Ireland'. Richard Bagnall, a porter or casual labourer engaged in work for Samwell, refers to 1599 the building of new structures and the consequent agreement, 'about two years past'. Hoppdale and Bagnall really agree with Samwell's reference to the summer preceding the previous summer, to paraphrase his reckoning, that is, again in 1599. The date is surely clinched by Samwell's cumulative memory of a date between Midsummer Day, 24 June, and St Bartholomew's Day, 24 August, during a period marked by the great training at Mile End and by the absence of Essex in Ireland. The great training of the citizen militia of London in response to the new Spanish threat took place from 27 August to 4 September 1599. In the same year, Essex left London for Dublin on 27 March and returned to London on 27 or 28 September. Samwell relates the making of the agreement more especially to the great training, and we may reasonably accept his recollection and date it towards the end of August 1599. This agrees closely enough with Hoppdale's St James's tide later in the summer of 1599. The date is important as fixing the period of the building of the enlarged new galleries in the yard. The lease itself could not have been made in Easter 1599 with effect for eighteen years from Christmas 1598. This would have extended Samwell's tenure to Christmas 1616, beyond the duration of Woodlif's lease from the Poleys, which terminated at Lady Day 1616. We are bound therefore to reject both Hoppdale's evidence that the agreement followed on St James's Day in the same year as the lease, and that of the Star Chamber Bill, and to accept an interval of a year before Woodlif parted with his interest in the yard and its theatre to Samwell.

[1] C24/290/3. Samwell describes himself as 'chandler', of the parish of Whitechapel without Aldgate, aged about twenty-three, on 11 June 1601. Elsewhere, in 1606, he describes himself as 'yeoman' of Whitechapel, aged twenty-eight (C24/327/61). He signs his name as 'Richard Samwell', adding 'per me' in 1606, in a clear, practised hand. His father was dead before he gave evidence in June 1601.

At this point in the affairs of the Boar's Head Inn and of its theatre, two men enter upon the scene who are already known to Elizabethan stage-history, Robert Browne and Francis Langley, though only Browne is known so far as having any connection with the Boar's Head, through Mrs Alleyn's reference to his death in a letter to her husband Edward Alleyn in October 1603.[1]

According to Chambers,[2] it is vain to attempt to identify Joan Alleyn's Browne of the Boar's Head, whom he obviously distinguishes by separate entry in his list of actors from the famous Robert Browne of Worcester's Men who spread the reputation of English acting in recorded tours in Holland and Germany from 1590 onwards. But there is no doubt that Browne of the Boar's Head was Robert Browne, that he was the leader of Worcester's Men and travelled with them on the Continent. Chambers's scepticism, in fact, rests upon the confusion of two Robert Brownes, father and son. As for Francis Langley, he figures largely in the history of the Bankside south of the Thames, as purchaser of Paris Garden Manor in 1589, and as builder and owner of the Swan Theatre in Paris Garden in 1594–5. He was the nephew of a Lord Mayor of London, and brother-in-law of the influential Clerk to the Privy Council, Sir Anthony Asheley. Some attempt will be made in a subsequent chapter to trace the careers of these two men involved in the history of the Boar's Head Theatre. Each of the two apparently took over the responsibilities of a speculator who had over-estimated his resources. And Langley, it might seem, was defrauded by Woodlif into the purchase of an interest in the inn-yard theatre with most of which he had in fact already parted to Samwell. It was entirely intelligible that Browne should be attracted by any proposal from Samwell that he should finance the building of structures necessary for the development of the theatre in the inn-yard, and take over Samwell's responsibilities in general. His company of actors, Worcester's Men, stood in need of a suitable and stable theatre, and everything pointed to a period of prosperity for them at the

---

[1] *Henslowe's Diary*, ed. R. A. Foakes and R. T. Rickert, 1961, p. 297. 1603 was a bad plague year, when in the summer playing was mainly restricted to provincial tours 'in the country'. Mrs Alleyn reports that Browne 'went not into the country at all' that year.

[2] *The Elizabethan Stage*, II, pp. 304, 445.

Boar's Head, with John Duke as their leading actor, and Thomas Heywood as their regular working dramatist. Richard Samwell found himself unable to meet the capital expenditure to which he was committed under his agreement with Woodlif, and went to Browne. Late in 1599, Browne and Samwell came to the agreement that Samwell's interest in the property should be conveyed to Browne, in return for Browne's provision of the cost of all the new buildings.

We may well wonder, indeed, whether there had not been an understanding between Samwell and Browne before Samwell's negotiations with Woodlif. They had certainly been partners in the sense that Browne had financed Samwell's expenditure upon the theatre buildings by important loans of money. When Samwell found himself unable to repay Browne's loans, and to meet further necessary expenditure, he and Browne agreed upon an assignment of Samwell's two leases, the original lease and the verbal lease, by a formal conveyance to Browne, who now became landlord of the inn and of its yard and theatre. The consideration for this transfer of interest is set forth in an Interrogatory in Chancery as £100 already provided by Browne and a further £260 to be paid by him to Samwell. Samwell's son, however, gives a different account of the instalments, though not of the total, in reply to this Interrogatory. According to him, Browne had already provided about £200 towards the cost of the new galleries, and now paid Samwell a further £160 or more as consideration for the assignment of his leases.[1] It will be noted that this goes far beyond the expenditure of £100 contemplated under Woodlif's lease of 1594 from the Poleys. He was present, he says, when the bargain was made between his father and Browne, and also when the documents were sealed which recorded the assignment of Samwell's interests to Browne:

> Richard Samwell growing indebted unto [Browne] for moneys which [Browne] had disbursed for him in setting up the said galleries or rooms, and for moneys which [Browne] had lent to and disbursed for the said Richard Samwell to the value of two

[1] C24/290/3.

hundred pounds or thereabouts in the whole, and being not able to make [Browne] satisfaction thereof, he the said Richard Samwell in consideration thereof, and of one hundred and three score pounds more or thereabouts paid by [Browne] to him, did by a conveyance in writing under his hand and seal assign and set over unto [Browne] all and every the said rooms and premises so to him demised as aforesaid and also the said galleries and rooms which he held by the said latter agreement or Lease Parole and all the right title interest estate and term of years, which he the said Richard Samwell then had to come of and in the same.

There is every reason for accepting his statement about his father's expenditure, as he was responsible for keeping the accounts and

by the appointment of his father and for him did keep the book of the expenses about the same viz. of the timber, nails, boards, tiles, laths, and other stuff which was employed about the galleries, together with the workmanship, and hath the same book still in his keeping.

The elder Samwell, in a Star Chamber suit of 1600, estimated his expenditure upon the galleries at £300 and more. It is apparent that these structures were built on an important scale. It is also apparent that Browne had been associated with Samwell in their building from the beginning, and we can hardly doubt that this leading actor and manager of Worcester's Men was largely responsible for their design and, in general, for the design of all structures related to stage-purposes in the yard of the inn. He was, after all, the expert, and the theatre was erected for his use. Woodlif's and Samwell's hopes of profit from their investment appear to have depended upon the tenancy of the theatre by Browne and his company.

It was perhaps a bold venture for Browne to commit himself to the investment of his private resources in money in the development of the Boar's Head Theatre, which led to his acquisition of the whole property for the considerable period of Samwell's lease. The leader of a company of actors, it might seem, would be more favourably situated if he were free to deal with a landlord of a theatre, and committed only to the payment of a suitable share in the receipts of the ensuing performances. But now Browne's money was locked up in one theatre, and his interests bound him to that theatre exclusively. It is true that theatres were hard to find in a safe place, free from the veto of the City. Whitechapel Street, beyond Aldgate, and in Middlesex, seemed promising, as the George Inn had appeared to Brayne. Yet there was no certainty. The Privy Council was always to be considered, and in 1580 they had forbidden Brayne's proposed theatre, even in Whitechapel. Much would depend here on the influence of the Earl of Worcester, patron of Browne's company. There were also, in the background, the shadowy but real rights of the Manor of Stepney, from which the Poleys held in customary tenure, and in fact those rights were invoked in the coming struggle for the theatre. He could no longer depend upon Poley's influence as Steward of the Manor. There was a new Steward, and a new Lord Wentworth who was seeking to increase his revenue from his Manor, as various lawsuits disclose. Warning notes, again, may have sounded in Browne's ears both in Shoreditch and on Bankside. The Curtain in Shoreditch had descended to be a subsidiary of the Theatre, which the Burbages and the Lord Chamberlain's Men, including Shakespeare, had demolished to rebuild it across the river on a site already held on Bankside, as the Globe. Landlords like Giles Allen offered no security. Francis Langley's Bankside venture, the famous Swan Theatre, had run into stormy weather over its production of *The Isle of Dogs*[1] two years before, and had been closed down.

There were, however, factors of importance on the credit side of this venture, apart from the crying need of Worcester's Men for a theatre in which to exercise their profession. To all appearance Browne had a safe lease of the premises, inn, yard, and theatre, until 1615, and was independent of the demands and caprices of landlords. The whole revenue of the theatre was at his disposal (except for Woodlif's remaining rights in the western gallery) to provide for the payment of his company of actors and for his landlord's share. The theatre was newly and handsomely equipped with stands for spectators, and with all the structures required by the actors for the

[1] See Chambers, op. cit., IV, pp. 453–5.

production of plays. It was equipped for winter use, an all-weather theatre, as appears in the evidence of John Mago.[1] Stage and galleries alike were covered structures. Finally, he had bound one of the most distinguished companies of Elizabethan actors to an agreement for occupancy of the Boar's Head Theatre under his management. The principal actors of Worcester's Men had entered into bonds to maintain this agreement and the company had begun to play at the theatre. With John Duke as their leading man, and Thomas Heywood as their dramatist, a prolific and successful writer of plays, attached to the Boar's Head, its success could hardly be doubted. And so the situation presented itself, not unreasonably, to Browne. The situation was, indeed, parallel in appearance as in date to that of the Lord Chamberlain's Men at the Globe in 1599. There too members of the company were landlords of their theatre, the theatre was newly built and equipped, and Richard Burbage, their leading man, and William Shakespeare, an outstanding dramatist, were powerful attractions to the London playgoer on Bankside, as were Duke and Heywood in Whitechapel. Browne might well nourish high hopes for his venture.

These fair prospects for Browne's theatre were, however, soon clouded over by what was surely the unforeseen intervention of Francis Langley as a rival claimant to the property, his claim deriving from a conveyance from Woodlif of his interests in the inn-yard and theatre. It would seem clear that Woodlif was engaged in driving two horses at the same time and in different directions. He entered upon his verbal lease of the yard and theatre to Samwell at the time when the construction of the new galleries was approaching completion and when Worcester's Men were about to enter into occupation. With these structures, the Boar's Head offered to the view a fine new large theatre which Langley might well, upon inspection, contrast with his tempest-tossed Swan Theatre on Bankside. If his purchase was valid, it was an attractive investment to all appearance. Langley paid Woodlif £400 for his interest in 'the inn called the Boar's Head'.[2] Of this sum £100 was paid in cash, and the remaining £300 was secured by three bonds of £200 each. Woodlif entered into a bond of 1,000 marks,

[1] C24/304/27, Interrogatory 14.
[2] C33/99/f. 464ᵇ, dated 6 May 1600. Requests 2/466, Part Two.

£666. 13*s.* 4*d.*, to complete the conveyance. Langley's counsel in Chancery defined the transaction as the purchase of 'a lease of an inn'. But Langley himself spoke in Star Chamber of buying Woodlif's 'whole interest in the inn'. The conveyance was drawn up and signed on 7 November 1599. It ignored all encumbrances upon the property other than the lease of the inn-premises to Samwell in 1598, and Woodlif evidently represented to Langley that the whole yard and all the theatre-buildings were at his disposal, as well as his parlour over the entry. If we admit the validity of the Lease Parole of August 1599, as we must, Woodlif's interests were in fact limited to half the profits of one gallery, with licence to occupy the parlour.

Langley's acquaintance with Woodlif and Mrs Woodlif had been brief. He had met them for the first time in the spring of 1599, as he told the Court of Star Chamber,[1] when he also met Samwell and presumably inspected the Boar's Head in Woodlif's company. As a result of this brief acquaintance, believing himself to have bought a lease of a theatre, he found a rival landlord in possession backed by a powerful company of actors.

It is difficult to shed tears for Francis Langley. As one follows his trail in the reflections of his activities in courts of law, where he is ubiquitous, the impression deepens of an unscrupulous financier devoid of integrity. His investment in Woodlif's Boar's Head was certainly precipitous and ill-advised. And it was perhaps the last venture of his chequered career. The Swan Theatre, in which he had sunk a good deal of capital, was shipwrecked. He laid down £300 to provide costumes and to refurbish the theatre, and bound Pembroke's Men to his service there, and for a time had a good return upon his investment. But in July 1597 the catastrophic production of *The Isle of Dogs* ended these halcyon days, and closed the theatre. He fought it out with the actors in law, and sought unavailingly to have his licence renewed, where Henslowe's Rose Theatre was more fortunate. The outcome was a heavy financial loss to Langley, with a theatre that was no longer an asset. When he came into contact with Woodlif and the Boar's Head, Langley was approaching the admission of disaster which was evident in his sale of Paris Garden on Bankside,

[1] Star Chamber 5, S13/8.

in which his Swan Theatre stood. The acquisition of Paris Garden in 1589 had been the climax of his career and the evidence of his success. But in 1600 he divested himself of the possession of this property and sold it to Hugh Browker or Brooker, who also bought from him lands held at Enfield.[1] He was unable even to satisfy Woodlif's demands for the Boar's Head without the backing of his nephew Richard Langley for the bonds securing the payment of the purchase-money.

It may seem strange that after Langley's lamentable experience of the Swan Theatre he should enter upon a further theatrical venture. But he had had seasons there of success and high profit. And he was no doubt attracted by the new field of Whitechapel. Bankside had its disadvantages, difficulty of access across the river, and strong competition from Henslowe's Rose Theatre. That competition was more than doubled by the advent of the new Globe Theatre with the Lord Chamberlain's Men, for whom it was available in the autumn of 1599 at latest. Neither the Swan nor the Rose, indeed, could well stand up to such a rival. Both buildings suffered from wear and tear and were going out of fashion. It is much more than a coincidence that upon the establishment of the Globe on Bankside both Langley and Henslowe embarked upon new projects, and that both deserted Bankside in favour of suburbs in Middlesex, north of the river. Henslowe and Alleyn decided to build their new Fortune Theatre in Golden Lane outside Cripplegate, and in December 1599 Alleyn bought land there for this purpose. In November of the same year Langley completed his purchase from Woodlif of the Boar's Head, with its new structures for actors and audience. Both theatres were sited in populous areas in rapid growth, and with comparative immunity from interference by hostile authority. No longer in the vicinity of the Lord Chamberlain's Men and their theatre, they could hope to obtain licences without opposition from them and from their powerful patron.

It is possible that Langley had thought of the Boar's Head as a home for Pembroke's Men, upon his resumption of his relations with them, broken by the loss of a licence for the Swan and by his law-suit with their leaders. But before his transaction with Woodlif was completed

[1] C24/305/1; C2 James I, B14/64.

in November 1599 Worcester's Men under Browne were already occupying the Boar's Head, and no company could offer greater prospects of profit for their landlord. Their attachment to the theatre may indeed have decided Langley to acquire it as a going concern. What he could not have foreseen, without more candour on Woodlif's part, was that effective control of yard and theatre had passed to Samwell and was about to be assigned to Browne, in the summer of 1599. The immediate result of his transaction with Woodlif was therefore no comfortable and life-saving revenue from a flourishing theatre, but a welter of conflict with Woodlif and with Browne which went far beyond mere legal controversy and which imported melodrama into the back-stage world of the Boar's Head Theatre.

Chapter *IV*

The Battle for the Theatre

The Legal Background

By November 1599 all the conditions were amply fulfilled for an outbreak of litigation on a grand scale, with a complexity of pattern proper to Elizabethan England's generous choice of courts having rival attractions and power to interfere with each other's proceedings. On the main issue, the title to the Boar's Head, interest was claimed by four conflicting parties, Samwell, his successor Browne, Woodlif, and Langley, each seeking to assert his rights not only in the inn but also in the profits of the company acting in its theatre. This conflict led in turn to the breach by Worcester's Men of their undertaking to Browne at the Boar's Head and to consequent litigation on this issue. All these legal proceedings, fortunately, reflect a good deal of the intimate history of the matters at issue, including episodes of violent action by Langley and a reign of terror at the inn.

Samwell opened the legal ball in Michaelmas 1599 with an action for trespass in Queen's Bench against Woodlif, and a simultaneous suit in Chancery against Woodlif and Langley to vindicate his possession of the inn and theatre. Langley, abetted by Woodlif and other accomplices, replied by direct and violent action in assertion of his rights in the theatre, as well as by more legal shifts to annoy Samwell. This gave material for Samwell's Bill in Star Chamber on 11 April 1600 against his persecutors. United as Woodlif and Langley stood against Samwell in pursuit of their common interest, they were divided against each other by Woodlif's failure to provide a clear title to all the rights he claimed to dispose of, Langley consequently withholding the purchase price. Civil war ensued. Woodlif sought to enforce payment by Langley upon his bonds at Common Law, and Langley appealed against him in Chancery, whose first decrees in the suit were issued in May 1600.

In the summer, or in the early autumn, of 1600 Browne moved against Worcester's Men, claiming the forfeit upon their bonds before Queen's Bench. Duke and Heywood and the rest sought relief in Chancery. Their Bill was presented, and Browne's answer sworn, in the Michaelmas Term. The court dealt with the matter in decrees of May and June 1601. After the acquisition of the inn from Samwell, Browne took further action in Chancery against Woodlif and Langley. His Bill was dated before 9 May 1600, though this suit did not reach the stage of depositions until June 1601. But Samwell was dead before June 1601, and Francis Langley died in the latter half of that year.[1] The suits in which they were concerned consequently lapsed.

Samwell's interests had passed to Browne, and Langley's to the executors of his estate, his wife Jane and his nephew Richard. Guerilla warfare now ensued between Woodlif and Richard Langley, and between Woodlif and Browne in various courts. About Christmas 1602 the bailiff of Stepney Manor seized the Boar's Head for Woodlif against Langley in a collusive action. In January 1603 the two closed their ranks by agreement in Chancery for Woodlif to resume the rights he had sold to Langley, and Browne and Woodlif once more came to grips. On 20 May 1603 Woodlif proceeded anew against Browne in the Court of Requests, and a Chancery suit by Browne against Woodlif and Richard Langley came to the stage of depositions in July. Later in 1603, during the grave plague epidemic of that year, both Browne and Woodlif died, and the stream of legal evidence concerning the Boar's Head dried up, though Langley's estate continued to keep the court busy with his other unhappy ventures, especially with Paris Garden.

With so redoubtable a litigant as Francis Langley, the pattern of this series of actions was inevitably complicated by diversionary

[1] *Editors note*: Herbert Berry, in the article referred to on page xii, suggests (p. 64 n.) July 1602 as the date of Langley's death. See also p. 73.

tactics conjured up from the underworld of law. He set up men of straw, Bishop and Wollaton, to sue the Samwells for trespass in Queen's Bench. He invoked the Marshalsea Court, in Woodlif's name, against the Samwells for disturbance of the peace. We cannot doubt that here Langley was exerting undue influence, the influence of his sinister brother-in-law Sir Anthony Asheley, brother of his wife Jane, and a Clerk to the Privy Council.[1] The Marshalsea Court, of course, could only properly deal with offences concerning the Queen's Household, but the Samwells had good reason to fear the elasticity of its jurisdiction. Arrests on both sides were numerous, and the Samwells became house-bound to avoid further arrests, complaining of no less than six miscellaneous suits levied against them by Langley. At one time or another every available bailiff came into action in these embroilments, the bailiffs of Marshalsea, of the Sheriff of London, of the County of Middlesex, and of the Manor of Stepney. But these minor litigations leave no trace of value to add to the information supplied by the main sources in Chancery, in Star Chamber, and in Requests.

Alarums and Excursions

The events reflected in these law-suits, as they affected life in the Boar's Head Inn, varied from the assaults and piratical invasions proper for consideration in Star Chamber to such material for comedy as is frequently recorded in the all-embracing scope of Chancery which dealt so largely in circumstantial and hearsay evidence in its search for full information. Its toleration of the trivial and familiar intimacies of life is illustrated in what might be called the Adventure of the Pump.

Late in the summer of 1599 Mrs Poley, in the exercise of her right to draw water for her own use in her rooms from the pump in the yard, sent her maid with a pail. In June 1601, Mrs Jane Harryson, wife

---

[1] For some taste of Asheley's quality, see C. J. Sisson, 'A Topical Reference in *The Alchemist*', in *Joseph Quincy Adams: Memorial Studies*, eds J. G. McManaway, G. E. Dawson, and E. E. Willoughby, 1948.

of Cuthbert Harryson, a goldsmith of St Botolph's near by, tells how she

> accompanied one Elizabeth the servant of Mrs Poley to the pump
> standing in the yard of the said tenement when she went to fetch a
> pail of water there and the pump being then broken she could
> have no water there, whereupon the said Elizabeth demanded of
> the wife of Oliver Woodlif one of the defendants how she should
> do for water, and how it chanced the pump was not mended,
> telling her that she well enough knew that her mistress was to be
> allowed water there, and not to be driven to seek it anywhere
> else, and she remembereth well that the said Woodlif's wife
> made this answer or to this effect, 'My husband hath passed over
> all to Samwell both yard and pump and other things, and
> Samwell must mend it, and my husband hath nothing to do with it,
> nor will meddle with it.'[1]

Her story, and her report of the conversation, are confirmed by an
older woman, Mrs Alice Saunders, who was then fifty-five years of
age to Mrs Harryson's thirty-two, and was the wife of Roger Saunders
of Whitechapel, a butcher, but free of the Drapers of London. She
too was in the yard at the time, but not at the later Affair of the
Rubbish, upon which Mrs Harryson supports the evidence of the
principal actor in this incident, Richard Bagnall of St Botolph's
without Aldgate, a white baker by trade but evidently a porter or
casual labourer by occupation, then aged twenty-six, who reports:[2]

> at such time as there were new galleries and a new stage made in
> the messuage or inn called the Boar's Head in the parish of
> White Chapel which he taketh to be about two years past, he this
> deponent was procured by the said Oliver Woodlif to carry away
> out of the yard of the said house certain rubbish which was cast
> under the stage, and after such time as he had carried away the
> same rubbish and had made clean the yard, he repaired to the said

---

[1] C24/290/3.
[2] Ibid. Richard Samwell the Younger varies the phrase to 'about the stage'. The
difference is significant. He probably reflects the final enclosing of the stage by
boards, whereas Bagnall reflects its earlier, unenclosed, condition, as does Mrs
Harryson. The existing stage was in fact being moved nearer to the hall of the inn.

Woodlif for his money for his work, thinking that he would have paid it him, because he set this deponent a-work. But he saith that when he asked the said Woodlif for his wages or hire, Woodlif made answer that he had nothing to do with it, and nor would pay him anything, willing this deponent to go to Mr Browne for it.

Bagnall's report would obviously date the affair after Browne had taken over from Samwell. But Mrs Harryson's version carries more conviction. She was, she states,

> afterwards present in the said yard when there fell out some controversy in speeches betwixt the said Richard Samwell and the said Woodlif about certain rubbish which then lay under the stage, and the controversy was which of them should carry it away, for Samwell would have had Woodlif to have been at the charge to carry it away, and Woodlif thereunto answered that the rubbish was the said Samwell's and that he the said Samwell was to be at the charge of carrying it away, and Samwell thereunto replied that Woodlif should bear half the charge. Woodlif answered he would not bear a penny of it whatsoever it came to, 'for', quoth he, 'it is yours and none of mine, and I will not meddle with it'.

It would be difficult to be more explicit. For us today the significance of such evidence lies in the certainty that a permanent raised structure stood as a stage in the yard, under which was a convenient space for the deposit of considerable building spoil. For the Court of Chancery its significance was the support given by credible witnesses to Woodlif's effective and public admission of the validity of his Lease Parole of the yard to Samwell. It may be that the Judges in Chancery found the Puzzle of the Rent even more compelling in favour of Samwell. For here Woodlif was not evading troublesome charges but went to the ultimate sanction of refusing to accept money offered to him in payment of rent from Mrs Saunders, who says that she

> and her husband do now hold and occupy a little piece of ground or garden plot, parcel of the ground belonging to the tenement or

inn called the Boar's Head in the said parish of White Chapel and
have so holden the same by the space of these twenty years and
above. And it was first let unto them by Mr Poley deceased, to
whom they continued tenants so long as he lived, and after his death
they held the same under Mrs Poley his wife for divers years
until such time as she demised the said messuage or tenement
unto the said Oliver Woodlif, after which demise they became
tenants thereof unto the said Woodlif, and paid him rent therefor
for some certain time, but how long she cannot now readily set
down, but it was until such time as the said Woodlif by report
had passed over his interest in the said tenement and premises
unto Richard Samwell mentioned in the Interrogatory lately
deceased,[1] and she saith that after such report she this deponent
demanded of the said Woodlif to whom she should pay her rent
for the said little garden or garden plot, and Woodlif thereunto
answered that she was to pay the same to the said Samwell,
saying that he had passed over all the said tenement or inn and
garden and his interest therein unto the said Samwell, and the like
report did the said Woodlif's wife make to this deponent and
others in her hearing. And she saith that she was present when
the said Woodlif did deliver possession of the said garden to the
said Samwell, taking the key of the garden of this deponent
for that purpose, and saith that after such possession-giving this
deponent and her husband did become tenants of the said garden
plot unto the said Samwell and paid him rent for the same.

There is no record of any formal giving and taking possession of the
yard such as Mrs Saunders describes in respect of the garden, but it
should be noted that Woodlif denied in Star Chamber that the garden
or back-yard was included in the original lease. On the evidence,
therefore, it was implicit in this denial that there was some subsequent
agreement upon its extension.

The interest of these peaceful back-stage exchanges, however,
pales before the more dramatic impact of Francis Langley's entry

---

[1] Mrs Saunders gave her evidence on 10 June 1601, and thus determines the
approximate date of Samwell's death.

upon the scene after he had purchased Woodlif's flawed interests in the inn, when the two men made common cause against Samwell's rights as lessee of both inn and theatre.

At the end of September 1599 there was good reason for expecting the fulfilment of Samwell's highest hopes and for a full return upon the capital he had sunk in the Boar's Head. The theatre was available for occupation, licensed by the Master of the Revels and protected at Court. Browne, who had furnished part of the capital by loan to Samwell, held the bonds of the six other principal sharers in Worcester's Men to play at the theatre in which he had this interest, and at no other. By Michaelmas they had begun playing, under their leader John Duke, with Thomas Heywood his fellow-actor and successful dramatist, and with Richard Perkins, soon to be a star of the first magnitude among Elizabethan actors.[1] The theatre, with its covered stage and roofed galleries, was designed and equipped for use as a winter theatre, and the resources of the inn were available for playgoers requiring food and refreshment. The Boar's Head indeed served admirably the needs of Worcester's Men, who were moreover Browne's fellows. They had come to the usual agreement with Samwell as landlord, though the box office arrangements were complicated by Woodlif's surviving right to his share in the takings of the west gallery. All went well for a while, with Woodlif apparently contented with the payments made to him and comfortably in residence with Mrs Woodlif in his parlour and chamber. But the situation changed shortly when Woodlif achieved the sale of his rights in the Boar's Head to Francis Langley on 7 November, by a transaction that ignored his Lease Parole of the yard and theatre to Samwell, for a price that reflected these wider interests.

The fur immediately began to fly, in the middle of a successful autumn season, with Langley in Woodlif's parlour as a foothold in the inn to pursue his claims to be landlord of the theatre in Woodlif's place. Woodlif, who had received £100 cash down from Langley and

[1] He describes himself as aged forty-four on 13 October 1623 (C24/500 and 501). The baptism is recorded in the Whitechapel Registers on 26 May 1583 of 'Richard Parkins', probably the actor, though this would make him only forty in 1623. He may have been the son of John Perkins of Leicester's Men in 1572–4, perhaps at the Red Lion.

awaited a further £300 secured by bonds, inevitably supported Langley's claims and denied the Lease Parole to Samwell. Samwell at once took the question to court, with an action in Queen's Bench for trespass against Woodlif, and a Bill in Chancery against Woodlif and Langley. He had the advantage that he was actually in possession of yard and theatre, and Langley judged that stern measures were called for, in which he himself took a leading part, to challenge that advantage. The sequence of events is somewhat uncertain in the welter of evidence from various sources and of varying dates. But Friday 13 December may be reasonably certified as the day of Langley's invasion of the theatre and its stage to assert his rights. An occupying force of seven, including two bailiffs of the Marshalsea Court, a carpenter Roberts, and two of Langley's servants, were led by Langley and Mrs Woodlif into the yard, when Samwell's carpenters were busy about the galleries for spectators, and overcame their resistance. The players, arriving for their performance, found to their consternation that the stage was occupied by armed men in an angry and threatening mood, under the leadership of a new claimant to be their landlord. The players, Worcester's Men, knew Francis Langley well enough, we may be sure, though they had never used his Swan Theatre, so far as we know. And they were aware that he had friends at Court and was a dangerous man. It seemed wise to them to give way to his demands, to ensure the peaceful continuation of their season at the Boar's Head.

Some three years later the incident was recalled and narrated by two trustworthy witnesses in Chancery.[1] John Mago, who describes himself as 'the chief carpenter and master workman' engaged upon the building of new galleries by Samwell, was there in the yard with his assistant John Marsh when

> Francis Langley or his assigns did by policy get and by force
> with some rude company keep the possession of the said stage
> and tiring house and galleries, swearing and protesting to kill or
> slay any that should resist them. . . . He with his man was working
> in the said great yard for the complainant at the time of the said

[1] C14/304/27.

possession-taking and before, and one of the said Langley's company with a halberd or such like weapon struck at this deponent's servant then working there and almost [maimed *deleted*] wounded him, but as God would he hurt him not.

John Marsh confirms Mago's account, remembering that Langley

got the possession of the said stage and tiring houses [sic] from the complainant, and with a company of rude fellows kept the same, some of them swearing and vowing that they would kill or murder any that should resist them. And this he hath cause to remember for that one of the said company with a halberd or such like weapon had almost maimed this deponent in the thigh, being then there at work for the complainant [Browne].

Both agree that 'so many extraordinary means wrought for getting of possession' pointed clearly to the absence of any valid legal claim. Mago reports the sequel: that upon Langley's

getting possession, and upon the vows and protestations aforesaid, some of the company of the players as this deponent hath heard were forced to enter into bond to pay £3 a week for a certain time, which they were constrained to do because Langley held the possession from Browne, and the players for that winter had no other winter house licensed for them to play in, and as he hath heard the said weekly payments began at Michaelmas time or thereabouts and were to continue until Shrovetide then next following.

Mago's information here was at second hand, of course, but is trust-worthy as coming to him from Browne, or Samwell, or the players. He was in close touch with both men as their contractor, and indeed later on backed some of Browne's bonds when Browne ran into the heavy charges of Langley's multiple litigations against him. Mago was evidently a substantial man of acceptable credit.

The significance of the players' bonds to Langley is not obvious at first sight, however. There is ample evidence that Samwell had kept to the terms of his leases from Woodlif and had kept up payments to him and afterwards to Langley of the rent of the inn and yard for Woodlif to meet the Poleys' claims, and also of Woodlif's half-share of the profits of the great west gallery since the playing-season began. On 7 November Woodlif had sold his rights to Langley, who therefore had no claim before that date. The players' bonds, we may reasonably think, were to take effect either from 7 November or from 13 December, and the period mentioned by the witnesses covered the playing season Michaelmas to Shrovetide, including the period from Michaelmas during which the half-share of the actual profits had in fact been paid by Samwell. The weekly payment of £3 was obviously an estimate of averages accepted by Langley and the players alike as reasonably representing half of a total of £6 a week from the great gallery. It is certain that Browne, as senior member of Worcester's Men and their manager, must have agreed to the signing of the bond by Duke and Heywood and others, and possibly by himself. The importance of the transaction to Langley was that it vindicated his position as the assignee of Woodlif's interests in the theatre, and it is probable that the bond was effective from 13 December and not before, at a time when dissension had already begun between Langley and Woodlif, about a month after Langley's purchase of Woodlif's interests.

It is certain also that before 13 December Browne had negotiated his take-over from Samwell of Woodlif's leases to him. Mago and Marsh state clearly that Langley's invasion was usurping Browne's established possession of the theatre, not Samwell's. He was therefore in the unusual position of being landlord of the theatre occupied by his own company. As late as in 1603 he is still described on behalf of Woodlif as a fellow of Worcester's Men. Their bonds to him to play exclusively at the Boar's Head, entered into in the summer of 1599, were therefore bonds by the chief sharers to their own leader or manager. It was an extraordinary situation, justified only by Browne's need of security for his heavy personal investment in the theatre for the good of his company, first by loans to Samwell and then by purchase of his leases. It may well be that the new bond to Langley rested lightly upon the company, as everything pointed to the explosion of a conflict between Langley and Woodlif in litigation, during which neither would be able to make undisputed claim to the rent of the inn or the profits of the galleries, a situation that eventually arose and from which Browne profited.

Certainly Langley did not content himself with the results of his blackmail levied upon the players, whether they paid or did not pay the weekly £3 to which they had become bound. He claimed interests extending beyond Woodlif's admitted half-share in the gallery, and his campaign spread to cover all opposition to his enjoyment of the lease of an inn which he maintained he had bought from Woodlif. Up to a point the Woodlifs were with him, in the hope of validating their transaction with him and of the completion of his payments to them of the purchase price of £400. It is plain that Langley, thanks to his relationship by marriage with Asheley, had the resources of the Marshalsea Court and to some extent of the Privy Council behind him. The venal Marshalsea Court offered procedures of prompt efficacy, as compared with the incorruptible and slow processes of Queen's Bench or Chancery, and Langley obtained warrants for the arrest of Samwell and his son at the suit of Langley and Woodlif. On 16 December, at seven o'clock in the evening, Langley led a second raid into the Boar's Head, forcing an entry, to execute the warrant. Some scuffling and violence ensued, subsequently interpreted by Samwell as attempts to murder him, and the Samwells took evasive action and escaped arrest that night. The immediate crisis was met by a visit to the Marshalsea to deposit securities for their appearance when required.

A week later, in the Christmas week, Langley's assaults reached their climax. On Christmas Eve he went with his gang to put Anthony Strayles in possession of the galleries to collect entrance money on his behalf for the play about to be performed. Langley then proceeded to make rapid structural alterations in the main gallery, breaking down its wall and opening up a new door which was accessible from Langley's parlour, through which he and his agents could enter and take possession of the entrance to the gallery. The younger Samwell protested, and resisted, but without avail. Langley's carpenter Owen Roberts completed the work under the supervision of Langley, Mrs Woodlif, and Strayles. Langley was thus in control for the per-

formance to a full house on St Stephen's Day, 26 December, and took
away £4 gathered by Strayles.

There was certainly no security at the Boar's Head. Langley
intensified his legal attacks upon the Samwells. He had set up Bishop
and Wollaton as assignees of part of his lease from Woodlif, and all
three proceeded separately with warrants of arrest for trespass from
the Marshalsea Court and the Privy Council, from which Samwell,
his son, his son's wife Winifred with her newborn baby, and his
servants Edward Willys and Rowland Rose all suffered, with heavy
fees to be paid for release from the Marshalsea prison. Langley himself
agreed in Star Chamber that the elder Samwell had been arrested once,
the younger twice, and Winifred once, by Foxley, Boulton, and
Johnson, bailiffs of the Marshalsea, during the Christmas season,
upon his instigation. The Samwells complained that this constant
repeated menace of bailiffs with warrants for their arrest obliged them
to keep at home within doors, the usual resource of Elizabethan
debtors and very hurtful to men's reputations. This period of violent
assault by Langley appears to have been brief, however. Many causes
may have contributed to his abandonment of such methods of pur-
suing his claims. Browne had replaced Samwell as the principal rival
to his pretensions to own both inn and yard, and Browne controlled
Worcester's Men, whose occupation of the theatre alone ensured a
regular return upon his investment. Langley could not wish to produce
such chaos as would forbid profitable playing in the Boar's Head and
put an end to his weekly £3 from the players. If Langley had friends
at Court, so had Browne, not least the Master of the Revels, who also
had a weekly revenue from Browne and his men of 15s. a week, in
addition to the £10 paid to him for licensing the theatre to them.
There was danger too of contempt of court, for Samwell had already
launched an action in Queen's Bench against Woodlif for trespass and
a Bill in Chancery against Woodlif and Langley to vindicate the
leases, which he had conveyed to Browne. Finally, Langley was
finding himself heavily engaged in a conflict with his ally Woodlif.
The Michaelmas Term ended with a welter of law-suits afoot, whose
issues would be deeply prejudiced against a litigant who persisted in
taking the law into his own hands.

A Flurry of Litigants

We may perhaps pause to consider the plight of Francis Langley, whatever we may think of his oppression of the Samwells. He had suffered a grievous loss at his Swan Theatre two years before, and it remained dead upon his hands, under an interdict, and doubtless in great disrepair. His deal with Woodlif, as he discovered, had not put him in possession of a new theatre, as he had believed, but only of some share in the speculative and uncertain profits of performances there, over which he had no control. For this, he was committed to the payment of £400. His multiple law-suits involved him in heavy expenditure. His finances were stretched to breaking-point and he was being pressed by large-scale creditors with whom he had been associated in his purchase of the Manor of Paris Garden. There was perhaps some measure of desperation in the violence of his proceedings at the Boar's Head, which were in the nature of a last throw of the hostile dice. He was in fact already preparing for the sale of Paris Garden with his great house there and his deserted theatre. For the moment, he had conveyed his interest in the Boar's Head to his nephew Richard Langley, who had stood bound with him to Woodlif for the payment of the purchase price, so that this asset was not now in his possession. Finally, there is the clearest evidence that Browne was taking advantage of the head-on collision that now took place between Woodlif and the Langleys, to withhold the agreed weekly payments to Langley. A decree in Chancery on 15 January 1601 reports a rueful statement by Woodlif's counsel Ayloff that 'one Browne, who is tenant of part of the house or inn in question, taketh the profit of the whole house and payeth nothing either to the plaintiffs [the Langleys] or defendant [Woodlif]'.

Early in 1600, in the Hilary Term, Woodlif had lost patience and proceeded at Common Law against the Langleys upon their three bonds to enforce the payment of £300 to complete the purchase. He himself had entered into a bond of 1,000 marks to effect the conveyance. The Langleys appealed at once to Chancery to adjudicate upon the matter and to stay Woodlif's suit at Common Law. Francis Langley, they agreed, had 'bought a lease of an inn' from him, but 'for his security of the lease he cannot quietly enjoy the lease by reason of encumbrances done by the defendant'. Our sole source of knowledge for these suits is the books of decrees and orders, but they are exceptionally informative, beginning on 6 May 1600, when we hear that Woodlif was prepared to cancel the whole transaction with Langley, to resume his lease of the inn, to return Langley's bonds in exchange for his own bond, and to refund the £100 paid down by Langley.[1] The court approved the settlement, subject to Langley's claim for the cost of repairs to buildings. The matter dragged on, after the fashion of Chancery suits. Langley had his injunction against Common Law proceedings, and was dilatory. Browne was imported into subsequent hearings, when the Masters in Chancery sought to find terms for a final settlement, as owing Woodlif £16. 18s. 8d. for recent repairs and buildings. The claim was later defined as a claim for a share in the profits of the house. Browne naturally protested that he was no party to the suit, and the Court contemptuously ordered that he should pay forthwith to Woodlif 'so much as he shall charge himself withal'. The proceedings continued on their inconclusive way in parallel with Browne's own action in Chancery against Woodlif and Langley to vindicate his rights in the Boar's Head by purchase from Samwell, a suit that was launched in Hilary Term 1600, though the depositions were not taken until Trinity Term 1601.

In the meantime something of a Nemesis overtook Langley and the Woodlifs in the shape of a Star Chamber Bill by Samwell, dated 11 April 1600, which could not be ignored and demanded immediate attention. Langley's Answer was sworn on 17 April, and other Answers followed on 24 April and 10 May.[2] Woodlif excuses this delay until 10 May by pleading that Samwell had, 'without any good cause', caused him 'to be arrested by a bailiff of Middlesex upon an action of trespass as he was coming to his learned counsel for the penning and engrossing of this his Answer'. True or not, this suggests the density of the legal traffic in which these parties were engaged.

---

[1] The decrees leave us in doubt whether the £100 was in fact paid down by Langley. They are in conflict one with another. One orders Langley to bring the £100 into court. Another reports that Woodlif's Answer to Langley's Bill offers to refund the £100.

[2] Star Chamber 5, S74/3.

Langley's Answer did not ward off the attack, and indeed it was evasive. He appeared before Star Chamber on 30 April and made his deposition upon full and detailed interrogations.[1] It is plain that Langley and Woodlif buried their own differences for the time in face of the common enemy, and consulted together as joint defendants against Samwell's attack. They were prepared to arrive at a compromise agreement to settle those differences, whereas no reconciliation could be sought with Samwell, whose claims were equally fatal to both.

Samwell's Bill, a formidable indictment, asserts his own rights as lessee of the Boar's Head Inn and its yard, and as builder of the theatre constructed in it at a cost of some £300, and proceeds to report the manifold attacks launched by Woodlif and Langley upon his lawful enjoyment of his rights, as also upon his own safety and liberty and that of his family and his servants. The offences include assaults, riots, false imprisonment, conspiracy, maintenance, and other abuses of the process of the law, all matters within the special purview of the Court of Star Chamber. Langley is the prime villain of the piece, indignantly cited by Samwell as

> being a man heretofore questioned and convicted in your
> majesty's high court of Star Chamber for many unlawful
> offences and being a man also well known to be a barrator and
> common disturber of your majesty's subjects by prosecuting
> suits by sinister vexation of your subjects and upon buying of
> many other pretensed rights and titles to lands and tenements
> and of divers debts.

This was no wild accusation. Langley had in fact appeared before Star Chamber on one occasion at least, as I can certify, for abuse of his office as Alnager of the City of London since 1587, and for exacting bribes from East Anglian clothiers in 1598–9, when Sir Edward Coke laid information against him. The case was tried in July 1599, less than a year before Samwell's Bill unkindly recalled it to the court's memory.[2]

[1] Star Chamber 5, S13/8.
[2] Star Chamber 5, A8/4; A25/27.

The Bill proceeds with a narrative of Langley's enormities from 13 December 1599 onwards at the Boar's Head, in a series of armed forays upon the inn and its theatre in which he was himself a leading figure. A forcible entry by night into the inn on 16 December ended with murderous assaults upon Samwell and his son, with daggers cast at them which stuck in the walls of the house, and reduced them to saving their lives by flight. On 24 December, 'then and there being a stage play', he usurped possession of the theatre with a raiding party which included Oliver and Susan Woodlif, when they 'most forcibly gathered and took away the money of those persons that were to go up into the said galleries to see the said stage play amounting to the value of four pounds or thereabouts'. On the final foray, immediately after Christmas Day, on 26 December, patronised by the implacable Susan, the raiders being accompanied by the carpenter Owen Roberts, Langley broke into the 'galleries and rooms and cut part of the said galleries down with axes and saws, and did break the doors of the said galleries'. A rueful catalogue of legal oppressions completes Samwell's complaint. Langley, on a fictitious complaint, had the Samwells bound to keep the peace in Queen's Bench, as a preliminary to his own intended assaults upon the inn. These assaults were combined with repeated arrests of the Samwells and their servants upon warrants alleged to be from the Privy Council and executed by Foxley and Johnson, servants of Sir Thomas Gerrard, Knight Marshal of the Queen's Household. Even Winifred, the younger Samwell's wife, with her three-weeks' old baby,[1] was carried off to the Marshalsea prison in Southwark, as were their servants Edward Willys and Rowland Rose. The Samwells obtained their freedom only by entering bail, and paying the Marshal's men heavy fees, £4 and £8 on various occasions. Suits were multiplied against the Samwells by setting up men of straw, holders of fictitious sub-leases from Langley, to complain in the Marshalsea Court of their eviction by Samwell. By all these devious means Langley had involved Samwell in legal costs so far of over £40, and had never sought a plain remedy at Common Law.

---

[1] The Parish Registers of Whitechapel record only the baptism of a second child on 24 February 1601—Sara, daughter of Richard and Winifred Samwell.

At the very time of Samwell's Bill, his son was once more in the Marshalsea gaol, held there without bail since his arrest on 4 April.

In their Answer, Alexander Foxley and John Johnson cloaked themselves in their duties as inferior officers of the Marshalsea Court, and agreed that in that capacity they had frequently arrested Samwell upon writs from the court, and taken fees for the Knight Marshal. The two Woodlifs denied that the inn-yard was ever leased to Samwell, who had no right to it. Their own title in it was lawfully conveyed to Langley. Nor was Samwell authorised by Woodlif in his spending of £300 upon the theatre. It was untrue

> that the buildings in the said great yard was limited forth by
> [Woodlif] to be built in the said great yard . . . for . . .when
> [Samwell] was in building and altering of the said galleries and of
> the sinks and gutters within the said great yard, [Woodlif] did
> forbid and forewarn [Samwell] and his workmen so to do.

As for the 'multiplicity of suits' complained of, Woodlif's smug defence is that this is not 'any offence, for that multiplicity of wrongs cannot otherwise . . . be righted'. He himself had recently been arrested by a bailiff of Middlesex upon an action of trespass at the instigation of Samwell.

The only depositions extant are those of Langley and Roberts, among the eight defendants cited, which we may consider along with their Answers. Langley appeared before the court on 30 April. No longer able to describe himself proudly as of the Manor of Paris Garden, he is now merely 'of St Saviour's, Southwark'. There are clear signs of failing health in the somewhat quavery writing of his signature, though he was hardly an old man. He was fifty-two years of age, the age, however, at which Shakespeare died, and they had been years crowded with intense activity and constant conflict. He stood up stoutly enough to the searching interrogatories put to him in the court, which covered step by step the validity of Samwell's title, the instigation and maintenance of a complex of suits against him, and the violence of his assertion of his rights in the Boar's Head premises. Interrogatories and depositions alike throw light on the history and structure of the theatre as well as on these conflicts of persons.

Upon enquiry as to Samwell's expenditure upon the stage and galleries in the yard, Langley was content to answer that the money spent on new galleries by Samwell was derived from receipts from existing galleries, and not from Samwell's own resources—an evasive reply which, however, certifies previous structures for spectators. The dangerous accusation of champerty and maintenance is rebutted by denial of Langley's complicity in the tangle of suits rehearsed. Bishop and Wollaton, Langley's lessees, acted independently, under direction of the attorney of the Marshalsea. Winifred Samwell was arrested by warrant from the Marshalsea for the offence of rescuing her father-in-law under arrest. Samwell was arrested four times about Christmas, but by Bishop and Wollaton, not Langley. It was not denied that six suits were then current against Samwell and his family and servants. He evidently felt on safer ground in dealing with his intrusions into the inn.

The yard and its galleries were in Woodlif's possession when Langley bought his rights on 7 November 1599. The affair of 16 December was merely a routine entry of officers of the Marshalsea, upon Woodlif's suit, to arrest Samwell, an arrest followed by his rescue on his way from Langley's house by his son and his servants, who assaulted the Marshal's officers and men. Langley, however, agrees that on 24 December at the Boar's Head[1]

he did set Anthony Strayles to gather money there of such as came then thither to hear the play and they did gather so much money as their part came to 5*s*. . . . and they did so gather the money for that the galleries were set upon [Langley's] ground.

He reports further upon a later similar incident on 26 December:

he did not gather or procure any money to be gathered or taken of any person or persons that came to the galleries to see the play upon St Stephen's day last past but he and Strayles did offer to gather money the same day of such as came thither to hear the

---

[1] Five shillings should not be taken as the whole sum gathered. It was the gatherers' share deducted from the total paid to their employer, Langley. This was Langley's wily attempt to minimise Samwell's assessment of the takings of £4. The gatherers' fee appears to be something like a shilling in the pound.

play but were resisted by Richard Samwell the younger, son to [Samwell] and the reason why they did so offer to gather money of such as came to the galleries that day was for that the galleries do stand upon [Langley's] ground.

The Interrogatory here refers to Langley, Strayles, Roberts, and Susan Woodlif standing 'there at the [stage *deleted*] gallery doors' to take money. This suggests several doors giving access to the galleries, with the main entry near the stage. It is to be observed that no reference is made to collecting money from spectators standing in the yard, whose payments would be made at the gate leading into the inn and its yard. It seems clear that the gallery-spectators were the principal source of the theatre's revenues. Langley's anxiety to ensure these takings was explicable, and was undoubtedly behind his forcible modification of access to the galleries, of which Owen Roberts, his carpenter, gave an account in his deposition. Two operations were carried out. In the first an existing door was forced:

> [I] was sent for by Langley to come to open a door at the stairs foot leading up to the said galleries ... [we] did set [our] hands to the said door and did thrust it open.

This was in preparation for Langley's gatherers to hold the entry for spectators. The second operation is thus reported by Roberts:

> about Christmas last [I] was commanded by Langley to cut down a wall and make a doorway into the galleries which [I] did accordingly with such tools as are necessarily used in such like works and no other ... there was none present at the cutting down of the wall but [me] and Langley ... as [I] was cutting down the wall [Samwell's] son came unto [us] and did forbid [me] to work there and thereupon Langley willed [me] to go forward in his work and he would bear [me] out in it.

Langley described the operation as cutting down certain quarters 'in the end of the galleries', and making a doorway into the galleries. The key to its purpose is contained in his Answer to the Bill, reporting his orders to Roberts to leave work he was engaged on for Langley in the inn 'and to go to cut down certain quarters and boards in the wall of the new gallery built in the great court, for to make a doorway from [Langley's] house into the gallery'. We have here the clearest evidence that the western gallery had been extended to adjoin the main buildings of the inn over the entrance gate, with its higher ranges level with the parlour and chamber on the first floor.

There is, as usual, no record of the outcome of the suit in Star Chamber, whose decrees and orders are not preserved. It may well have been inconclusive, and possibly not persevered with by Samwell. The main issue, after all, was possession of the inn and its theatre, and this issue was soon to lie between Browne and Woodlif, instead of Samwell and Langley. In the early summer of 1600 the courts had to deal with the tangle of three streams of litigation, Samwell in Star Chamber, Browne in Chancery, and Woodlif against Langley also in Chancery. It is not surprising that Chancery decrees show some confusion between its two suits on the same issue and the parties concerned. Langley, moreover, was deeply engaged on matters of greater import while these suits were afoot, the sale of his Manor of Paris Garden and other property, and was in financial straits and in poor health. Browne had his troubles with his company of actors, and was about to proceed against them on their bonds to him. At the end of the year they too went to Chancery against him in reply. Browne's suit against Woodlif and Langley lay dormant until next year, 1601. We are perhaps apt to forget that the active pursuit of court cases involved a constant expenditure of money for fees to lawyers, to the court, and to the court's officials, which could not be met by bonds, the Elizabethan equivalent of modern hire-purchase devices.

At all events, the situation changed in 1601, with the death of Samwell before June, and of Francis Langley later in the year. After Samwell's death Browne moved afresh in his Chancery suit with full depositions, before Langley died. In the October of the next year, in the course of clearing up Langley's estate, his nephew and executor Richard Langley revived his suit against Woodlif. He was himself financially interested in the matter, as joined with Francis in the transaction with Woodlif. He and Woodlif proceeded jointly at Common Law against Browne to recover from him possession of the yard and theatre, with failure in several such actions. Woodlif was more successful against Langley, and at Christmas 1602 obtained an *elegit* or extent from him of the Boar's Head, probably by collusion between them as an indirect method of gaining possession from Browne, for in the following month, January 1603, they had agreed upon arbitration and a final settlement in Chancery on the basis of Woodlif's offer of 1600 to cancel his lease to Langley, to withdraw all bonds, and to resume his rights in the Boar's Head. These rights, as against Langley, were asserted at Christmas 1602, when Woodlif's *elegit* was executed by the bailiff of Stepney Manor, who took possession of the yard, its stage and galleries, on his behalf. This was no doubt a symbolic seizure, and not maintained in Woodlif's actual tenure. The lists were now cleared for a duel between Woodlif and Browne, and each mounted a fresh horse in renewed litigation. Suits were launched simultaneously, by Woodlif in the Court of Requests, and by Browne in Chancery again. Woodlif's Requests Bill of 20 May 1603,[1] and Browne's Depositions of July,[2] are among the most illuminating documents of the whole series.

It is perhaps significant that Woodlif sought recourse to the Court of Requests, a poor man's court, though his claims upon Browne went far beyond the normal limit of financial issues in this court. But these far-reaching claims were really setting the stage for the immediate purpose of the suit, which was to obtain relief from Browne's Common Law pursuit of Woodlif's bond to him for payment of £16 in respect of building costs at the Boar's Head, on which Browne had had him arrested for non-payment. His Requests Bill recites once more the history of the Boar's Head leases, and maintains once more the position that the inn-yard was never leased to Samwell nor to his lessee Browne. Browne had merely usurped possession of the yard and of the theatre erected in it. The Bill specifies precisely the accommodation and layout of the inn, so that we can compare Woodlif's account in 1603 with the description furnished by Browne to Chancery in 1600. We learn also from Woodlif that when he made his lease to Samwell in 1598, Samwell was the occupier of the whole inn. Clearly

---

[1] Requests 2/466, Part Two.
[2] C24/304/27.

he was the innkeeper under the Poleys. Woodlif also reports weekly payments by Browne to Langley of over £5 as his share of the profits of the theatre and Browne's failure to continue these payments since August 1601.

Browne's renewed Chancery suit of 1603 was directed against Woodlif, Richard Langley, and one Henry Sibdall whose part in the affair is obscure. The evidence adduced in his depositions of July is devastating for any denial of Woodlif's Lease Parole of the yard and theatre to Samwell. Taken in conjunction with the earlier depositions of 1601, it can leave no doubt in our minds, and it must have satisfied the Court of Chancery. The evidence of John Mago, the master-carpenter engaged by Samwell upon the theatre buildings, and his chief workman John Marsh, is the precise, circumstantial, detailed, and decisive evidence of eye-witnesses of the transaction. They were fully aware of the considerations upon which this further lease was granted to Samwell, and by him in turn to Browne.

John Mago was present in the yard of the inn when Woodlif made the Lease Parole, to cover the period of the written lease and of Woodlif's main lease from the Poleys. It extended to 'the great yard of the said tenement or inn and also the new galleries which were then already builded or afterwards to be builded with the profits that should arise of them by any ways or means'. Mago's servant John Marsh, a carpenter also employed by Samwell on the work, reported in court an agreement between Woodlif and Samwell that Samwell should 'together with the premises demised to him as aforesaid have and enjoy also the stage, the covering over the stage, the tiring houses, and the galleries over the stage during the years contained in the said indenture of lease'. Both parties, said Marsh, seemed contented and pleased, and Samwell performed all that he promised in the agreement until he conveyed all his rights to Robert Browne. The buildings were agreed by Samwell and Woodlif. Marsh remembers Woodlif going round with a rule to measure the ground to be covered by the galleries. After much discussion it was agreed that

Woodlif should have the moiety or half of the profits of the galleries over the stage and at one end of the stage which

Woodlif had built (the gatherers being first paid) and the players the other half.

The burden of running-costs of the theatre was transferred to Samwell, and was heavy, as both carpenters agree. According to Mago's account of the matter it was a principal consideration of the Lease Parole that

> Samwell the elder or his assigns should pay or cause to be paid all these charges following, that is to say, for all warrants or licences to the Master of the Revels which by their report cost £10 a licence and his weekly payments which was affirmed to be 15s. a week when they played, and the weekly payments to the poor in regard of playing which was said to be 5s. a week, and for rushes and cresset lights in winter which some weeks came to ten or twelve shillings a week, as they said, and for the wages to the stage keepers, which was said to be 6s. a week, and for all charges of suits at court to uphold playing in the said house, which came to much money, and that the said Samwell should discharge the said Woodlif of the charges which the said Samwell in Woodlif's absence bestowed in the repairing of the stage and tiring houses which came to twelve or fourteen pounds or more.

The agreement was made 'in the great yard of the said inn when the great new galleries were in building in the yard next the parlours, in which building [I] was the chief carpenter and master workman'.

Four points of interest and of some difficulty arise in Woodlif's Request suit. There is firstly the allegation that Browne has prevented Woodlif, for lack of access, from carrying out his covenant to the Poleys to execute building work to the amount of £100, and has thus imperilled his grand lease of the inn and his bond of £300. The covenant had in fact expired on 27 November 1601. Woodlif's own statements in his Bill, moreover, speak of his expenditure upon the galleries as agreed upon in the negotiations upon the return to him by Langley of his rights, and as undertaken to satisfy his covenant with the Poleys. Certainly there is no indication of any termination of the grand lease by the Poleys, whose main concern was the rental of £40 payable upon the lease, before its expiry in 1616.

Secondly, his complaint of the cessation of weekly payments from

Browne due from 22 August 1601 onwards suggests this as the date of the death of Francis Langley.[1] It clearly is not explained by the decree in Chancery of 15 January 1601 which reports a similar complaint. It might of course be the date of the opening of a playing-season at the Boar's Head, but this seems doubtful. It is apparent that the return to Woodlif of the rights in the inn sold to Langley became effective only after the death of Francis and was executed by Richard. It was sanctioned by Chancery in 1602, and implemented by Chancery in a decree of January 1603. Browne in his Answer to the Requests Bill maintains that Woodlif had received from him all that was due up to Michaelmas 1602 from rent and half-profits. Any profits due from Michaelmas 1602 to March 1603 and retained by Browne amount to under £6, and he is ready to account for this to the Court. There is no doubt about the significance of these dates. In March 1602 Worcester's and Oxford's Men were joined in a licence to play at the Boar's Head, and began their winter season there in Michaelmas. On 19 March 1603, playing was stopped by the Council upon the fatal illness of Elizabeth, and continued in suspension after the accession of James because of the outbreak of the dreadful plague of 1603–4.

The third point is the emergence of a minor character of interest, Israel Jordane, who is described by Woodlif as 'of London, scrivener, belonging unto Browne and his fellow stage players', and as Browne's adviser in his plots against Woodlif. Browne's Answer reports a loan of £4 from Jordane for Woodlif's benefit, for which Browne gave a bond. This specific description of Jordane certainly suggests that he was the scribe and book-keeper of Worcester's Men, and perhaps their treasurer. If so, one cannot envy Jordane his task of writing fair copies and actors' parts from the execrable manuscripts of the company's chief dramatist, Thomas Heywood. Finally, there is no doubt whatever about Browne's status in May 1603 in relation to the company. Woodlif's Bill describes him as 'a common stage player', and speaks of Browne and his 'fellow stage players'. Browne's Answer refers to 'this defendant and his fellows'. It is clear that in 1603, as twenty years before in 1583, he was a sharer in Worcester's Men, soon to be Queen Anne's Men.

[1] See p. 51 n.

There is no record of the outcome of these last suits. No relevant decree was passed in Chancery after the final order of 28 January 1603 which preceded them and which appointed Justice Walmesley as umpire for the details of Woodlif's repossession of his title to the inn-yard. But this of course only settled the matter as between Woodlif and Langley. Browne's Bill and depositions of 1603 again challenged that title and reduced it to a half-share of the main gallery profits, and there can be little doubt that he established his case. It is certain that the cases came to a halt when the courts closed their Trinity Term sittings upon the dangerous increase of plague in the summer of that year, in which, moreover, both litigants died. Woodlif was buried on 30 July, and Browne on 16 October, both in the churchyard of St Mary's Whitechapel. All four claimants to enjoyment of the lease from the Poleys were now dead, Samwell, Francis Langley, Woodlif and Browne, and all suits had lapsed that debated their respective titles. The battle for the theatre had ended, with Browne in undisputed possession of the inn and its yard and theatre, and with Richard Samwell the younger his manager of the inn.

The End of the Story

We may pause to consider the value of the lease from the Poleys in Browne's hands at the time of his death. The one unchanging feature of the situation was the annual rental to the Poleys upon which continuation of the lease depended and for which Browne was responsible. Forty pounds a year was a considerable sum to find. Added to this were the running costs of the theatre, which amounted to some £2 a week during the playing season, and the levies of the Master of the Revels and of Court officials. Performances at the Boar's Head had long been troubled by Langley and Woodlif and by the disloyalty of members of Worcester's Men, and the theatre was entirely closed, along with others, from March 1603 until after Lent 1604, because of plague. Payment of the rent to the Poleys could be assured only by profits from the inn until the theatre could open again for playing. Browne no doubt enjoyed also, as a sharer in the company, some part of its profits on tour in the provinces. The long litigation, as Browne complains, had exhausted his means. He could only subsist from hand to mouth, it might seem, and there is every reason for accepting Mrs Alleyn's report to her husband that Browne of the Boar's Head died very poor.

Little remains to be added to the history of the Boar's Head after Browne's death. What estate he possessed passed no doubt to his widow, the redoubtable Susan, who continued to figure largely in the affairs of Browne's company of actors, now Queen Anne's Men, during the next twenty years. From Browne she would inherit his lease of the inn and its yard, valid until 1616, and his share in the company, probably a one-seventh share. She was about twenty-five years of age, with a family of five young children by Browne, and she soon found a second actor-husband, Thomas Greene, to succeed Browne at the inn and in the company. It was a sensible arrangement. The company did not have to find the money to pay off the capital value of the share but simply transferred the share to a new sharer.

Greene's name is first recorded as a member of the Queen's Men early in 1604, towards the end of the list of those granted cloth to appear in the coronation procession. But in an undated draft licence, evidently of the same date or thereabouts, his name heads the list. He was clearly the leader of the company in August 1604 when 'Thomas Greene and ten of his fellows ... the Queen's Players' attended as grooms of the chamber at Court.[1] He first appears as payee for Queen Anne's Men for Court performances, in succession to John Duke, at Christmas 1608. The last previous payment, however, was at Christmas 1605. It seems certain that Greene married Susan within a few months of Browne's death, and joined the company as a sharer and as its leader in his place, after Lent 1604 when playing was permitted again at the Boar's Head as elsewhere. Greene would be a notable addition to the company which in 1602–3 had certainly had the services of the famous clown, William Kemp, for it was as a clown that Greene made his great reputation, and Kemp appears to have left the company after 1602–3 or may have died. In the well-known later suit between

[1] Chambers, *The Elizabethan Stage*, IV, p. 170.

Susan and the company in 1623[1] Greene is described after his death as 'one of the principal and chief persons of the said company, and a full adventurer, storer and sharer of in and amongst them', and Susan claims that he advanced £37 for the company's outlay. He died in 1612. So long as the company continued at the Boar's Head after the reopening of the theatres in 1604, he would apparently succeed Browne as their landlord. There may well have been further changes in the composition of the company after Browne's death. It appears probable that they moved to the new Red Bull Theatre upon its opening in 1606, and that Greene disposed of the Boar's Head, or rented it, to John Garland and the Duke of Lennox's Men, a new company formed in 1604.

Certainly the Boar's Head emerges again in 1608 as occupied by the Duke of York's (Prince Charles's) Men, described then on a visit to Leicester as 'the Prince's players of the White Chapel, London'. This description distinguishes the company plainly from 'the Prince's players', the Admiral's–Prince Henry's–Palsgrave's Men, by reference to their London theatre. The company was formed in 1608, and appears to have absorbed the Duke of Lennox's Men, led by John Garland, after its brief life from 1604 to 1608. Garland led the Duke of York's Men in 1610, when their licence permitted acting 'in and about our City of London' as well as in the provinces. It may well be in fact that the theatre was occupied from 1604 onwards by Garland with Lennox's Men, followed in 1608 by the Duke of York's Men. The Lord Mayor complained in April 1607 of the need for supervision of acting in, especially, Whitechapel, Shoreditch, and Clerkenwell, surely in reference to the Boar's Head, the Curtain, and the Red Bull.[2] The evidence is not conclusive, but no other theatre is known to have been available in Whitechapel. A numerous family of Garlands appears in the Whitechapel Registers. In 1576 John Garland was married to Joan Heron, and Thomas to Margaret Lancaster in 1578. In 1605 John is recorded in the Henslowe papers[3] as resident in Old Ford, which is close to Whitechapel, and in 1618 he is listed as a

---

[1] Chambers, op. cit., II, p. 237.
[2] Chambers, op. cit., IV, p. 339.
[3] Chambers, op. cit., II, p. 241.

tenant of Stepney Manor.[1] It may reasonably be believed that Garland took over the lease of the Boar's Head from Susan and Greene, until its expiry in 1616.

The end of the lease may be seen to be reflected in the history of the Prince's Men and their amalgamation with Lady Elizabeth's Men in a group which on 20 March 1616 agreed with Alleyn and Meade to occupy the Hope on Bankside.[2] It is probable that Mrs Poley's heir, Sir John Poley, found it more profitable to develop the buildings and site of the Boar's Head, or to dispose of it to a speculator, for other purposes than those of an inn and a theatre, in the rapid growth of this residential and industrial suburb of London. He may, of course, have granted a renewal of the lease to Garland, who was still a tenant of the Manor in 1618, but this list suggests copyholders rather than lessees. We may reasonably close the history of the Boar's Head as a theatre with the expiry in 1616 of the Poleys' lease of 1594 to the Woodlifs.

[1] *Customs of the Manors of Stepney and Hackney*, 1675, p. 46.
[2] Chambers, op. cit., II, p. 245.

Appendix A

The Inn-yard Theatre in Chambers, Lawrence and Hotson[1]

It is desirable to review the principal previous accounts of the inn-yard theatres and their stages, as a background to the views here expressed. Chambers surveys the whole field of Elizabethan theatres, including inn-yard theatres in London with a more detailed account of what is known about the great City inn-theatres, the Bell, the Cross Keys, the Bull, and the Bel Savage. Their importance in the history of the stage is manifest, and Chambers quotes Flecknoe's reference in 1664 to the actors who at the beginning of Elizabeth's reign 'set up theatres in the City in the inn-yards' of the Cross Keys and the Bull. It is clear that Chambers contemplates the galleries of the upper floor surrounding the yard as available for spectators, the actors' tiring room as provided in some ground-floor room of the inn, and an upper stage in some part of the gallery. But his practical imagination led him to conceive the probability that the landlords of some inns exploited their use as theatres by 'structural alterations which in fact converted their yards into little less than permanent theatres', and he refers to the 'play-scaffolds' at the Red Lion in 1567 as supporting this suggestion.[2] It is indeed implicit in the precise wording of Flecknoe's statement, and I had the pleasure of discussing with Chambers at a later date the new evidence which bore out in full the prophetic suggestion which he 'read between the lines'. In the way of

---

[1] J. Stinson's 'Reconstructions of Elizabethan Public Playhouses', in *Studies in the Elizabethan Theatre*, ed. C. T. Prouty, 1961, leaves out of account the history and structure of inn-yard theatres and stages. The survey, with its reproductions of the chief pictorial designs, is invaluable in other respects.

[2] Chambers, *The Elizabethan Stage*, II, 1923, pp. 356–7.

his early full acceptance of the theory stood only imagined concepts of the logic of the basic original structures of inns as serving the purposes of occasional performances without serious interference with the normal business of an inn. This prevented also any serious consideration of the inn-yard theatre as influential in the design of public theatres built from the ground for this exclusive use. For Chambers, moreover, the weight of de Witt's use of the word *amphitheatre* in relation to the London theatres has laid an emphasis which told against any pattern derived from rectangular inn-yards in favour of circular designs, though the Globe was probably polygonal and the Fortune entirely rectangular. But taken as a whole Chambers's account of the London theatres, with his invariable freedom from dogmatism, leaves the way more free than his principal successors for reconsideration of the development of theatres in the light of new information.

What might perhaps be called the classical view of the inn-yard theatre is set forth by W. J. Lawrence in his influential book.[1] His account of a typical inn-yard rests largely upon W. H. Godfrey's sketch of the New Inn at Gloucester, deriving from Britton's engraving.[2] Here the main buildings of the inn are shown over the exit-gate from the yard, as also the main outside staircase. These features of the structure, yielding windows, stairs and an exit, were used as ancillary to the temporary stage set up in front of them, the players taking possession of these buildings. The galleries of the chambers served for spectators. We may well find difficulties in this account. It is extremely unlikely, in fact, that the New Inn was thus arranged before modern times, the normal pattern of an inn, for many excellent reasons, showing its hall, parlours, and tavern in association with the entrance gate, and stables and barns at the exit end of the yard. But the crucial feature of Lawrence's inn-yard theatre is the elementary stage proper to its occasional use by visiting companies of actors, with improvised use of inn buildings to eke out these slender resources, with stairs, inner stage, upper stage, and windows. It is true that he contemplates some kind of a permanent stage as useful

[1] W. J. Lawrence, *Pre-Restoration Stage Studies*, 1927, Chapter 1.
[2] J. Britton, *Picturesque Antiquities of the English Cities*, 1836.

equipment for an inn dealing with carriers' wagons and their loads. But the sharing of an inn-yard with the normal and established traffic of carriers is essential to his account.

A permanent stage set up against the exit-gate is certainly inconsistent with this concept of joint use of the yard in rotation by players and by carriers and their wagons. He accepts the provision of some seating constructed in the yard, in addition to accommodation for spectators in the galleries surrounding the yard. This was set up by the landlord of the inn and yielded his share of the profits from the performances. This too offers difficulties in the way of full use of the yard by carriers, unless the stands for spectators were removable. The stage, finally, included no structure to be used as tiring rooms behind it, and therefore had no entering doors in the stage wall.

Dr Hotson, in his *Shakespeare's Wooden O*, derives the inn-yard stage immediately from the long tradition of the pageant stage. His stage, indeed, consists of pageant-wagons. Permanent stages, he argues, would forbid the use of the inn-yard by carriers. The solution is removable pageant-stages rolled in only on playing-days. These are, in fact, the players' wagons, and he rejects the view that their function was to convey the actors' luggage, costumes, and properties on their provincial tours. These pageant-stages would permit of the continuance of the elaborate provision of 'houses', properties, and trap-doors which characterised the miracle plays. The actors thus provided their own stages, even as a circus-company raises its main and subsidiary tents, with benches for spectators, all transported in the company's wagons. Dr Hotson conceives of two pageant wagons, set end to end, furnishing a sizeable stage, each section in two stories. The enclosed lower storey serves as a tiring room for the actors, with internal ladders leading up through four trapdoors on to the visible stage with its 'houses', each provided with further ladders from the stage. This kind of structure, in his view, is the basis also of a public theatre like the Globe, so that his concept of the inn-yard theatre is inextricably bound up with this view of the London public stages. It is essential to his concept, as with Lawrence, that the theatre, inn-yard or public, has no inner stage in the accepted sense. It would be inconsistent with the pageant-stage and with a theatre in which a circle of spectators surround the stage on all sides, the stage occupying the centre of an arena. The well-known sketch of the Swan Theatre, he points out, shows no opening in the back wall of the theatre. And the transportable pairs of pageant-stages are derived from the traditions of the English miracle plays and vouched for by the practice of the Spanish stage. Mass-movements, as for battle-scenes, are provided for by a ramp giving access from the arena on to the stage and off it. Dr Hotson's theatre is not, in fact, a true 'theatre in the round' like a circus arena, for his stage has its back to a sector of the galleries, and projects into the arena.

This account of the Elizabethan stage, linking up the medieval pageant with the inn-yard and with the Spanish stage, has been found attractive by men of the present-day theatre in search of novelty as a counterblast to the enclosed picture-stage long established in the professional industry of the drama. The 'arena stage' in various shapes has been the basis of many experiments in England as in North America, and has led to productions of originality and interest. But few, if any, have found it possible to accept this account as representing the actual physical characteristics of any Elizabethan theatre, as being consistent with known facts concerning them, or as emerging from any new evidence adduced in its support. It has, of course, been pointed out that this imaginative concept presents insuperable difficulties of a practical nature.

The long progresses of a touring London company through the provinces, trundling heavy, lumbering, two-storied pageant-wagons along the difficult roads of Elizabethan England, cannot be certified by the example of carriers' wagons of lighter structure. The stage proposed, with cellarage, houses, ladders, four trap-doors, and various curtains manoeuvred by stage-hands, is a producer's nightmare of complexity and confusion. The cellarage tiring room allowing five feet from floor to ceiling, a dim tangle of ladders, is plainly denied by common sense, as also by the Swan drawing which shows the *mimorum aedes* behind the stage wall, evidence only evaded by arbitrarily interpreting the phrase to mean 'property-dock'. Indeed, a cellarage tiring room could only be adequate for the simple needs of a Punch and Judy team, and the evidence for structural tiring rooms is ample and documentary. As for the inner stage, rejected *in toto* in the arena stage, it is an absurd misunderstanding of its function in the Elizabethan stage to define it as a 'pigeon-hole' in the 'imaginary scenic wall'[1] as if action were limited in it only within the line of the stage wall, with a taboo laid upon any movement from this focus to the main stage. Other features of the stage give no less rise to questionings, the numerous stage-sitters on this busy and crowded platform accepted as normal for all performances, the constant intervention of uniformed and masked stage-hands drawing or closing curtains on the 'houses', or the orientation of the action of the play directed solely towards the lords' room above the stage. The picture as a whole is manifestly impossible as an interpretation of the actual physical conditions of any known or conceivable form of professional stage or theatre, or of the buildings in which it was operating.

In his brief discussion of the Boar's Head, resting upon my article of 1936 and upon examination of some of the relevant documents, Dr Hotson ignores all that is not in accord with his theory. The yard had galleries on all sides, the theatre is therefore a 'circus-theatre', he concludes. No account is taken of the evidence for the construction of a tiring house, or of the means and need for provision for inner stage scenes. His limited enquiry into the archives underlying the article did not unfortunately bring him into touch with the evidence of the carpenters who built the theatre concerning its structure. Their evidence, with that of others, is decisive.

It could hardly be expected that the evidence would bear out Lawrence's picture of a typical inn-yard theatre, as Lawrence is concerned with inns active in their normal functions harbouring occasional performances by travelling companies in conditions of improvisation. Dr Hotson's discussion of inn-yard theatres also assumes the sharing of inn-yard facilities between theatre-companies and carriers and the general business of an inn. With the Boar's Head, we are dealing with an inn converted into a theatre as a permanent home for a company of actors. It is important to place the theatre in its proper perspective, some twenty years after the building of the Theatre in Shoreditch, contemporaneous with the building of

[1] Leslie Hotson, *Shakespeare's Wooden O*, 1959, p. 153.

the Globe on Bankside and of the Fortune in Golding Lane, its history linked up with that of the Red Bull in Clerkenwell and of the Swan in Paris Garden, and serving the needs of one of the principal companies of actors, Worcester's—the Queen's Men. The evidence provides no support for Dr Hotson's theories concerning public theatres, and is in general consonance with the more conservative views emerging from the continual re-examination of the material already available by a group of able commentators in recent years.

Appendix B

Brayne, Burbage and Miles

The intervention of Robert Miles in the affairs of John Brayne gave rise in due course to much litigation of documentary value to historians of the Elizabethan stage, as Wallace's account of the fruits of his enquiries proved. But his interpretation of the material leaves much to be desired, and has affected injuriously all subsequent accounts of the association of John Brayne with Miles and with James Burbage. Fuller explorations of the field of documentary evidence confirm the impression that Wallace placed too much dependence on the case presented by Miles on his own behalf, with consequent falsification of the roles of Brayne and Burbage in the development of the London professional theatre.

It is part of Miles's case against Burbage that Brayne was an unwilling and deluded partner with Burbage in the foundation of the Theatre in Shoreditch, and was induced against his will to speculate in that venture and indeed to foot practically the whole bill for its erection, a victim of the assiduities of an actor with no means of his own. It is impossible to doubt, on the contrary, that Brayne was not only an enterprising speculator in the theatre, but was deeply interested in its possibilities and, perhaps, even in the art of the stage and drama. The known attraction which the stage had for the 'prentices of London crafts and commerce did not necessarily cease to affect them when they came to maturer years and greater means. Brayne's three ventures into theatre-building, the Red Lion in 1567, the Theatre in 1576, and the George in 1580, give ample evidence of this continued and active interest. It is probable indeed, as has been suggested above, that the Red Lion venture was a family affair undertaken in collaboration with Burbage and with the company of actors of which he was the leader, Leicester's Men. Burbage, it will be recalled, had married Brayne's sister Ellen, and their first son Cuthbert had already been born. What we might call the Wallace-Miles version of the relations between the two men presents Burbage as a man of no means, an unsuccessful joiner turned player, and equally unsuccessful and impoverished in his new occupation. It is difficult to conceive a prosperous grocer like Brayne marrying his sister Ellen to a man of no means, no standing, and no prospects. Nor is there any basis other than the prejudicial evidence of Miles for the limitation of Burbage's financial contribution to the Theatre to the derisory total of £50.

A share in the theatrical venture in Shoreditch was to Elizabethan eyes a most promising investment. The theatre business brought in immediate cash returns on every playing day, and cash was a scarce and valuable commodity, as none knew better than Miles. The theatre had something to sell for which there was a wide and eager demand among the growing population of London, swollen by the changing tide of those whose affairs brought them into the town from all quarters of the kingdom, drawn in by commerce or by the universal network of London courts of law in term-time. The outlook for the traffic of the theatre was reasonably favourable, especially in an accessible suburb beyond the City limits. James Burbage, moreover, was expert in the trade. He had a company of actors of quality and of some stability. Not least, he had a powerful protector in the patron of his company, the great Earl of Leicester. What such protection could mean his sons were to experience in the long legal battle with Miles, when Cuthbert Burbage invoked the decisive support of his influential master Sir Walter Cope, who spoke for the Lord Admiral.

We have every reason to view with suspicion all statements made by Miles in the course of his long and vindictive litigation with the Burbages, in which he sought every means open to him to prejudice the courts against them. He accused them, for example, of blasphemous language and, more dangerously, of expression of contempt for the courts and for established authority. But nowhere does his account ring more falsely than in his picture of Brayne as a deluded victim of Burbage in the foundation of the Theatre.

We should not conclude that as Burbage took no share in Brayne's further venture in the George Inn relations between the two men had degenerated. There was no good reason why Burbage should thus extend his investments. His concern was with a company of actors and a theatre for their use. It was quite enough to be landlord of the Theatre. Brayne was a speculator. And he may well have wished to be, like Burbage, the landlord of a new theatre, and not merely a sharer in profits. Certainly the two men were on terms of financial support from Burbage on Brayne's bonds as late as 1584. Taken as a whole, the facts available point to amicable relations between them in the difficult finances of the Theatre in its early days, and to an unhappy breach in those relations upon the death of Brayne in 1586 with the intervention of Miles behind the scenes in the first place and then, after the death of Margaret Brayne, in his own person.

I see no good reason for doubting the general picture of the course of events presented by Burbage in his Chancery Bill of 1588 against Mrs Brayne and Miles, with its clear interpretation of Brayne's participation in the Theatre as intended to ensure the advancement of his nephews and nieces, Burbage's children, being then childless himself.[1] The Bill makes it no less clear that the chief new element in the situation, Brayne's association with Miles in the George Inn, was decisive. It is true, of course, that other new elements were the deterioration in Brayne's fortunes and the apparently late and unexpected birth of his daughter Katherine.

It is reasonably certain that Brayne's primary interest in the George Inn venture came to an end a few months after his acquisition of the lease, when he was forbidden to proceed with the building of his intended theatre there. It is intelligible enough that he should seek a partner to reduce his commitments in a now burdensome speculation and to manage and develop the property for other purposes. His assignment of a half-share in his lease involved Miles in responsibility for half the rent payable to Field and half the costs of repairs and

---

[1] C. W. Wallace, 'The First London Theatre', in *Nebraska University Studies*, XII, 1913, pp. 39–45.

rebuilding, and we need not consider as probable the payment by Miles of any purchase-money whatever. Miles was to give his whole energy to the management of the joint property of both, a task for which Brayne had no relish now. There is good reason for questioning the picture set up by Miles of one capitalist coming to the help of another, and for giving more serious credence to Mrs Brayne's account of their association in her suit against Miles in 1587[1] than to Miles's various accounts in his suits in Chancery and Star Chamber. According to Mrs Brayne, after Brayne took possession of the George, Miles sought his help as an old friend, 'in his poor and low estate that he was lately fallen into'. He stood in great need of some housing for his wife and his four or five children, and he offered his services in return in the exploitation of the lease. He hoped thus to have some settled abode and to begin to pay off his debts. Brayne agreed to this, and the subsequent partnership in the lease in July, attributed by Mrs Brayne to compassion, and by Miles to purchase at some uncertain price, is understandable otherwise. Miles was then a man of forty years of age,[2] and obviously had given up his trade as goldsmith, if indeed he had ever exercised it after his admission as Freeman of the Company.

It is certain on the evidence of John Symes that the George was an inn in custom when Brayne and Miles took it over, though the buildings were decaying and custom was being lost.

It is to be noted that Giles Allen as late as in 1600 could describe Miles as an innholder of Whitechapel (Wallace, p. 251). The first recorded transaction of the partnership was the supplying of hay for the inn. Miles, unable to provide his half share of the cost in cash, offered the lease of the inn as security to his uncle George Scott of Chigwell, who dealt in hay. To satisfy Scott, Miles had to produce the lease, and induced Brayne to make a fictitious and temporary assignment of the whole lease to him. Supplies to the value of £40 were obtained, a quantity indicating the large scale of the ostlery side of the inn's activities. In June 1581 the purchase of other stock was financed by Miles by assigning the lease to John Banbury for £60.

[1] C2 Eliz. B13/5, April 1587.
[2] Aged fifty-two on 30 July 1592 (Wallace, op. cit., p. 139).

Miles's cousin, Robert Scott, who was also his lawyer, paid Banbury off in return for the transfer to Scott of the assignment. Brayne thereupon redeemed the lease at a cost of £93, with money received from a Sussex debtor, John Ashburnham,[1] but Scott in fact transferred it back to Miles. This is Mrs Brayne's story in 1587.

Miles tells a variant story in a Star Chamber Bill of 1593. The whole lease of the George was assigned by Brayne to Miles on 20 May 1581, and Miles mortgaged it to Banbury for £60. The lease was forfeited for non-payment of the loan, and conveyed by Banbury to Nicholas Bishop, a fishmonger. We meet Bishop again later as an agent and employee of Miles. But from Miles's opponents on the trial of the suit we learn that Anthony Leigh lent Miles £50 on the security of the lease in 1589, so that Miles had clearly re-entered into the lease. Leigh conveyed the interest to John Symes and Francis Oliver. Miles also conveyed to Symes the garden-plot of the George, on 13 August 1591, at a rental of 33s. 4d., despite the mortgage on the whole property. Oliver, a salter, set up there a vinegar factory. It is a tangled story indeed, with some notable gaps in probability.[2] Miles's main contribution seems to have been the hawking around of the lease as security for loans of money.

Another version of the story, offering even greater difficulties, and inconsistent with the first, is offered by Miles in 1605 in his action in Chancery for a renewal of the lease of the George refused by Nicholas and Bridget Bestney, heirs of John Field, upon its expiry in January of that year.[3] This maintains that Brayne assigned the whole lease over to Miles in consideration of money received from him, the price being stated on the conveyance. The date of the conveyance was 'eighteen years ago' in Hilary Term 1605, that is, early in 1587. This offers the obvious difficulty that Brayne had died in August 1586.

---

[1] See also State Papers Domestic Elizabeth I, CXLVI, 31, which contains signed statements by Brayne and Miles.

[2] Star Chamber 5, M17/25, M28/36, M31/35. Miles, Ralph Miles, and Bishop *v* Leigh, Symes and Oliver. Miles's *Replication* is signed by his lawyer, whose name is Scott. No consideration for Brayne's assignment is alleged. The assignment, as Miles says in his Bill, was a 'deed poll'. Brayne therefore had no copy, and the assignment involved no covenant on Miles's part. Bishop was now a 'soapboiler' and partner with Ralph Miles.

[3] C24/314/85.

His will, drawn up in 1578, naturally made no mention of the George Inn. And there is no doubt that the two men were on very bad terms at the end of Brayne's life. Wallace quotes an account of a Coroner's inquest upon him, which alleged manslaughter against Miles who had assaulted Brayne.[1] The date of 1587, nevertheless, is confirmed by two of Miles's witnesses, William Morgan, a Whitechapel carpenter, aged forty-one, and Ralph Dudley, a Whitechapel labourer, aged eighty-four, both employed by Miles at the George. Two of Miles's children, however, appear to question the date. According to his son George, then a mariner of Plymouth, aged thirty-seven, the conveyance was made in 1583. According to his daughter Elizabeth, wife of John Patteson, glazier, of St Mildred's, aged thirty, it was made in January 1581, and her date was agreed by Nicholas Bishop, aged forty. George would have been thirteen years of age in 1581, and Elizabeth six. Their evidence suffers accordingly. Brayne was certainly a partner and part-owner of the lease in July 1584, when Field made to them jointly a lease of the garden-plot behind the yard of the George, measuring 107½ feet wide by 34½ feet deep, for a down-payment of £30 and a token rental of 4d. a year.[2] In August of the same year Brayne and Miles jointly, as lessees of the inn, leased to James Norman the Mill House, part of the property, with ground adjoining behind the inn, for fifteen years at a rental of £5,[3] and Norman set up there a soap-boiling industry. After a legal battle, Norman was ousted, and by 1592 Bishop and Miles's son Ralph were partners in the soap-factory. It is clear that the lease was redeemed for Miles to engage upon further mortgages. Mrs Brayne gives a probable account of the redemption by Brayne, and maintains that Brayne paid the whole rent of £40 for three years, and spent £240 upon repairs and new buildings, despite covenants for Miles to provide half these expenses. Upon Brayne's death in 1586, Miles expelled Mrs Brayne from the inn, and as sole landlord secured the payment of all rents from its tenants to himself. A year later Mrs Brayne presented a Bill against Miles in Chancery.

[1] Wallace, op. cit., pp. 14, 86, 88. This rests solely upon the evidence of Henry Bett, the stoutest of pro-Burbage witnesses.
[2] Requests Eliz. 151/26. Robson v Myles. October 1588.
[3] C24/203/71; C24/204/Norman v Myles. Michaelmas 1588.

Brayne's fortune had certainly descended to a very low ebb by November 1584, exhausted by the George Inn, and in heavy debt. In a Requests suit[1] of that year he describes himself as 'of late greatly decayed, and indebted by reason of suretyship for others'. The suit is of interest as a reflection of the underground world of the book-trade. Christopher Amis of Stepney owed Roger Ward £15 for goods purchased from him, and Brayne backed the debt by his own bond of £30 to Ward. Brayne sought release from Ward, who found another surety in his place, John Clarke, and undertook to cancel Brayne's bond. This was arranged at a drinking party, presumably at the George Inn, as a happy gesture by Ward in return for his host's pots of beer. But by 1584 Ward was in difficulties. He was in fact in Ludgate prison, and from thence was sueing Brayne on the bond still uncancelled, though Amis had paid him and the goods had been delivered.

Roger Ward was, of course, the notorious pirate stationer. There can be no doubt that Amis was buying a parcel of some of Ward's pirated books, the sale of which must have offered problems. His secret presses had been at work certainly since 1582, as the records of the Court of the Stationers' Company show. They were seized and broken in 1586, 1590, 1591 and 1596. Brayne's Bill records the imprisonment of Ward in 1584, doubtless by the exercise of the powers of the Company, as again in 1586 according to the Court Book. It is amusing to recall that the most famous pirate at sea of this period was of the same name, the much-feared Captain Ward, who operated in the Mediterranean from Tunis.

This deep conflict of evidence, and the marked discrepancies in Miles's case, offer salutary warnings. The truth seems more likely to be nearer to Mrs Brayne's account of the matter. George Miles and Morgan accepted Miles's claim to have spent £500 on repairs and building tenements to let. But we may well see Miles as the active manager of the affairs of a partnership, both partners raising money as they could. All we learn about Miles precludes any idea that he commanded financial resources of his own, as Brayne undoubtedly did. Miles was certainly in effective control by assignment of the whole

[1] Requests Eliz. 181/47; Bill dated 9 November 26, Eliz. 1584.

lease at some time after 1584, probably to facilitate its use as security for loans or for the disposal of parts of the property on under-leases.

Two years after Brayne's death, Miles mortgaged the lease to Henry Anthony, a scrivener, redeemed it six months later, then mortgaged it afresh to Anthony Smith. Throughout the history of his management we have a constant picture of a desperate need of credit. The lease was apparently his principal asset. No wonder that when the lease expired in 1605 he went to great lengths to seek to enforce an alleged promise of renewal from Field's heirs, though without success.

It may seem strange that Margaret Brayne, opponent of Miles in respect of the affairs of the George Inn, was joint-defendant in 1588 with him when Burbage moved in Chancery upon the affairs of the Theatre, a year after Margaret's Bill against Miles. For Burbage, the death of Brayne removed the partner whose claims he admitted. These claims might reasonably be extended to his widow. But it was apparent that she was in the power and control of an alien speculator, Miles. As for Margaret, her action against Miles surely lapsed upon the initiation of Burbage's attack upon her share in the profits of the Theatre, and she naturally made common cause with Miles in the defence of an asset of far more immediate value than her dubious share in the affairs of the George Inn. Burbage knew well enough that his real opponent from the beginning was Miles, who in due course succeeded legally to Margaret's claims upon the Theatre. Margaret Brayne's will, made on 8 April 1593 and proved by Miles on 3 May, left to him her interest in the profits of the Theatre, and all her other property and chattels, in consideration of her great indebtedness to him for sums of money beyond the value of all her possessions.[1] This will merits close study, closer than the Probate Court gave it in 1593. It bears all the signs of dictation by Miles. No provision whatever was made, except in the goodwill of Miles, for Katherine, the daughter of John and Margaret Brayne. Great pains were taken to make sure that the will stood probate, with consideration alleged and with no less than five witnesses. Of these, John Patteson was Miles's son-in-law, and Nicholas Bishop was Miles's employee, his agent for the collection

---

[1] Commissary Court of London, Register 1592–7 (Guildhall Library), p. 26.

of Mrs Brayne's share in the takings of the Theatre, and joint-manager with Miles's son Ralph of the soap-factory in the Mill House. Barbara Bishop, a third witness, was his wife. Miles was the executor. Nothing could be plainer than that Miles had proceeded in his piracy of Brayne's assets from the annexation of the George Inn to the acquisition by undue influence of his rights to a share in the profits of the Theatre. And Burbage was aware of all this.

Miles's dealings as Brayne's partner, then his supplanter, in the George Inn venture, came in a measure to trial in 1605 with his suit to establish a promise by Field's heirs to extend the lease. From these unsuccessful proceedings he emerges without a shred of reputation or respect, even from his own children. The picture of the whole property given by James Norman and others is that of a lamentable slum area dominated by a contentious, oppressive, and penurious speculator. Of its original function as an inn, only a victualling-house remained. The tenants joined in opposition to the renewal of his lease. All had suffered law-suits at his hands. Nicholas Bestney, husband of Field's daughter and heiress, Bridget, brought irresistible evidence to this effect. Miles's son Ralph, now dead, had denied on his death-bed that any promise of renewal had been made. His daughter Elizabeth, married to John Patteson, recounts the many oppressions of her father, and his especial anger that she would not testify to any such promise. She recalls her father's attempt to intimidate her: 'thou wilt remember it when thou comest to thy oath, or else I will send thee to God or the devil.'[1] Nicholas Bishop, once Miles's representative to the Burbages, and indeed once 'challenged to the field' by the Theatre's outraged leading man, Richard Burbage, was a damning witness against Miles, who had pursued him also with law-suits to his great cost.

Miles ceased to trouble Whitechapel in 1614. He died there at the age of seventy-four, between 22 March 1614, when he signed his will,[2] and 8 April, when his widow Agnes obtained probate. Of the four children for whom he sought a refuge with the Braynes in the George Inn in 1580, the eldest, Ralph, had died certainly before 1605, and

1 C24/316/9.
2 P.C.C. 31 Lawe.

probably in 1603 during the great plague of that year,[1] at the age of thirty-seven. George, born in 1568, was apprenticed, as was Nicholas Bishop, to William Allen, carpenter, and was his servant in 1588–9. In 1605 he describes himself as 'mariner', of Plymouth, but he came soon to reside at Wapping with his wife Elizabeth and his son Robert. He signs his name in a practised hand. Elizabeth, born in 1575, wife of John Patteson, glazier, and Catherine, wife of Richard Sowersby, were his daughters, and these three children survived him.

It would seem that when we last meet Miles in Chancery in 1605 he was a friendless and ruined man, and his will reflects this condition. It was witnessed only by his scrivener and by his servant Agnes Pinner, who made her mark, a very different affair from the galaxy of witnesses he recruited for Mrs Brayne's will. Leases held by him in Whitechapel and in St Katherine's near the Tower were left to his wife Agnes for life, then to Edmund Stubberfield, goldsmith, subject to the payment by him of legacies of £10 each to Miles's two daughters and his grandson Robert, 40s. to George's wife Elizabeth, 3s. 4d. to George, and 20s. to Agnes Pinner. It would seem plain that these leases formed the whole of his estate with no assets to provide immediate legacies, and that their capital value amounted approximately to the value of these bequests to be provided by Stubberfield, some £33 in all. Miles's law-costs, of course, must have been prodigious over a lifetime of litigation.

He was, beyond all question, an inveterate and unscrupulous intriguer and litigant, and by all accounts a disagreeable character, who revolted even his own son and daughter. John Symes, a grocer of standing with whom he had dealings, complained of Miles's 'daily railings and exclamations' which sought to discredit Symes's reputation. It was typical of the man that even on his death-bed he vented his spleen beyond the grave upon his surviving son George with a derisory legacy of 'three shillings and fourpence and no more, because he hath been otherwise very chargeable to me.' And he died, still

---

[1] Whitechapel Parish Registers. 'Mr. Myles', buried 19 October. The burials recorded of 'Robert Myles', 1 September, and 'Mrs Myles', 17 October, may be those of an otherwise unrecorded first son and first wife. But all may be irrelevant.

raising money upon leases, in what was in effect a post-mortem assignment to Stubberfield.[1]

It is a grievous thought that such a man should have intervened so deeply in the affairs of the founders of the great stage that provided a setting for the dramatic art of Shakespeare, and that his evidence has coloured so strongly the accounts hitherto accepted of the affairs of the Theatre. I can find nothing to his credit except that his intervention provided one further irritant cause of the reincarnation of the Theatre in the great Globe Theatre on the Bankside.

[1] Miles's will indeed offers some pretty complexities to legal curiosity, a witness who is also a legatee, a diminishing asset sold at an indeterminate date, and no provision for the demise of the principal residual legatees.

Further Reading

There have been signs recently of increased interest in inn-yard theatres. Besides the writings referred to in the Introduction, the following may be consulted.

G. E. Bentley, *The Jacobean and Caroline Stage*, seven vols, 1941–68. The author discusses the Boar's Head in volume 6 (1968), saying that, although the theatre is outside his normal terms of reference, the evidence provided by Sisson and Hotson since the publication of *The Elizabethan Stage* obliges him to consider it. (He was writing before the publication of Herbert Berry's article.) He explains that he has been seriously handicapped in attempting to assess the evidence 'because neither scholar has yet published transcripts or full analyses of his documents'.

O. L. Brownstein, 'The Saracen's Head, Islington: A Pre-Elizabethan Inn Playhouse', *Theatre Notebook*, XXV, 2, pp. 68–72. The author refers to Sisson's 'important discovery in the mid 1930s of the Boar's Head documents', which 'has gone virtually unnoticed'. This article is concerned with the perfomance of plays at the Saracen's Head in 1557, the same year as the first recorded performance at the Boar's Head.

O. L. Brownstein, 'A Record of London Inn-Playhouses, *c.* 1565–1580', *Shakespeare Quarterly*, XXII, 1, pp. 17–24. In this article, Dr Brownstein examines 'The Register of the Masters of Defence' (B.M., Sloane MS.2530) as 'the only systematic account of activities of any kind at four of the earliest Elizabethan playhouses during the period of the origin of these playhouses. The Register records the places used by fencers for their "prizes" (degrees of rank within the fencing brotherhood) from about 1540 to 1590; in the last twenty years of this period the fencers had turned almost exclusively to the first permanent city inn-playhouses and to the first suburban theaters.'

In his final footnote, Dr Brownstein refers to Barbara Hubbard's M.A. thesis, 'Documents of the Boar's Head', University of Iowa, 1970. This was prepared, he kindly tells me, from his microfilms of the documents cited by Sisson and Hotson. No copy of the thesis appears to be available.

Richard Hosley, 'The Playhouse and the Stage', in *A New Companion to Shakespeare Studies*, edited by Kenneth Muir and S. Schoenbaum, 1971, includes discussion of inn-yard theatres, and a drawing by Richard Southern of a booth stage set up in an inn-yard.

S.W.

Index

Adams, J. Q., 20, 22
Allen, Giles, 45, 87
Allen, John, 8n., 18
Allen, William, 93
Alleyn, Edward, xviii, xx, 4n., 7n., 8,
    20, 42, 48, 77
Alleyn, Joan, xx, 20, 42, 75
Amis, Christopher, 90
Anne of Denmark: Queen Anne's
    Men, see Worcester, Earl of
Anthony, Henry, 91
arena stage, 81
Ashburnham, John, 88
Asheley, Sir Anthony, 42, 52, 60
Ayloff (lawyer), 62

Bagnall, Richard, 41, 53-4
Banbury, John, 87, 88
Baskerville (later Browne, then
    Greene), Susan, 7-8, 75-7
Beeston, Christopher, 9, 34
Bel Savage Theatre, 78
Bell Theatre, 78
Berry, Herbert, xi–xiii, 51n.
Bestney, Bridget, 88
Bestney, Nicholas, 14, 88, 92
Bett, Henry, 89n.
Biggs, John, 13
Bishop, Barbara, 92

Bishop, Nicholas, 88, 89, 91-2, 93
Blue Boar Inn, 22
Boar's Head Theatre:
    early history, xvii, 20-9
    inner stage, xviii–xix
    later history, 75-7
    layout of rooms, xii–xiii, xx,
        28-35
    location, 21-4
    management and finances, xix, 9,
        58-61, 67-8, 71-5
    position of stage, xiii
    structure and accommodation,
        29-35
    structural adaptations, from 1594
        to 1599, 35-49
    upper stage, xiii, xviii–xix
Boulton (bailiff), 61
Brayne, Ellen, see Burbage, Ellen
Brayne, John, xviii, xix, 4-6, 9, 10,
    11, 12, 13-19, 27, 45, 84, 86-91
Brayne, Katherine, 86, 91
Brayne, Margaret, 12, 17-18, 86-93
Britton, J., 79
Browker (or Brooker), Hugh, 48
Browne, Henry, 28-9
Browne, Robert, xviii, xix, xx, 7-8,
    20-1, 33, 35, 42, 43-6, 49, 50,
    51, 54, 56, 58-63, 69-75